Jaime Chamorro Cardenal is a top editor of *La Prensa*, the independent Nicaraguan newspaper with which his family has been involved for decades. His father, Pedro Joaquín Chamorro Zelaya, became owner and publisher of *La Prensa* in 1932. The following year, Antonio Somoza Garcia became head of the Nicaraguan National Guard, marking the onset of the Somoza dictatorship, which *La Prensa* opposed from the beginning. After the death of their father in 1952, Pedro Joaquín Chamorro Cardenal succeeded him as editor of *La Prensa*, and soon after Jaime Chamorro Cardenal began what is now over three decades of work at *La Prensa*. During that time he has worked in all aspects of the newspaper—editing, business and news-reporting. When Pedro Joaquín Chamorro was murdered, he was succeeded by his son, who was director from 1978 until his exile in 1984, at which time Jaime Chamorro assumed that post.

Jaime Chamorro Cardenal was editor of *La Prensa* when the newspaper was shut down by the Sandinista government of Nicaragua on 26 June 1986. He left Nicaragua for Costa Rica in September 1986 and stayed there until his return to Nicaragua in August 1987. *La Prensa* was granted permission to reopen and begin publishing again in September 1987 and the first edition of the newspaper was published 1 October 1987.

LA PRENSA

The photograph on the preceding page shows a wall on the *La Prensa* building after having been defaced by Sandinista supporters. The translation is, "The people want confiscation [of *La Prensa*]. Sandino lives. The battle continues. People Power. Criminal agents of the CIA. Death to La Pren(CIA). Bourgeois traitors."

LA PRENSA
The Republic of Paper

Jaime Chamorro Cardenal

FREEDOM HOUSE

Copyright © 1988 by Freedom House

Printed in the United States of America. All rights reserved. No part of this book may be used or reproduced in any manner without written permission except in the case of brief quotations embodied in critical articles and reviews. For permission, write to Freedom House, 48 East 21st Street, New York, N.Y. 10010.

First published in 1988.

Cover design by Emerson Wajdowicz Studios, N.Y.C.

Library of Congress Cataloging-in Publication Data

Chamorro Cardenal, Jaime.
    La Prensa : the republic of paper / Jaime Chamorro Cardenal.
      p. cm. — (Focus on issues ; no. 5)
    Includes index.
    ISBN 0-932088-24-4 : ISBN 0-932088-25-2 (pbk.) :
      1. Prensa (Managua, Nicaragua)—History. 2. Press—Nicaragua--History. 3. Press and politics—Nicaragua—History. 4. Nicaragua-Politics and government—1937-1979. 5. Nicaragua—Politics and government—1979- I. Title. II. Series: Focus on issues (Freedom House (U.S.)) ; 5.
    PN4989.N6Z954 1988   88-24295
    079 .7285—dc19   CIP

Distributed by arrangement with:

National Book Network, Inc.
4720 Boston Way
Lanham, MD 20706

3 Henrietta Street
London, WC2E 8LU England

Contents

Preface

I.	From the Beginning through the Somozas	1
II.	The Sandinistas in Power 1979-1980	15
III.	The Institutionalization of Repression	33
IV.	Assault on *La Prensa*	43
V.	Who Killed Pedro Joaquín?	65
VI.	Censorship, the Church, and *Vende Patrias*	77
VII.	Orwell in Nicaragua: Elections, Harassment, and Representative Censorship	89
VIII.	Revolutionary Tourism, Spies, and Tapped Telephones	99
IX.	The Beginning of the End	107
X.	Silence—and the Revolution Within	127
	Epilogue	147
	Appendices	151
	Index	185

FREEDOM HOUSE

Freedom House is an independent organization that places human freedom in the broad context of individual rights and global politics. Freedom House believes that civil rights at home and advocacy of human rights abroad depend upon American power, its prestige, and its human values.

In international affairs, these values concentrate our attention on violations of human rights by tyrants on the right as well as the left of the political spectrum. At home, our values stress the need to provide all citizens equality of opportunity, not only in law but in daily civic and private performance.

Freedom House has a very active program that includes bimonthly and annual publications, public advocacy, press conferences, lecture series, and research of political rights and civil liberties in every country.

About the Author

Jaime Chamorro Cardenal is a top editor of *La Prensa*, the independent Nicaraguan newspaper with which his family has been involved for decades. His father, Pedro Joaquín Chamorro Zelaya, became owner and publisher of *La Prensa* in 1932. The following year, Antonio Somoza Garcia became head of the Nicaraguan National Guard, marking the onset of the Somoza dictatorship, which *La Prensa* opposed from the beginning. After the death of their father in 1952, Pedro Joaquín Chamorro Cardenal succeeded him as editor of *La Prensa*, and soon after Jaime Chamorro Cardenal began what is now over three decades of work at *La Prensa*. During that time he has worked in all aspects of the newspaper—editing, business and news-reporting. When Pedro Joaquín Chamorro was murdered, he was succeeded by his son, who was director from 1978 until his exile in 1984, at which time Jaime Chamorro assumed that post.

Jaime Chamorro Cardenal was editor of *La Prensa* when the newspaper was shut down by the Sandinista government of Nicaragua on 26 June 1986. He left Nicaragua for Costa Rica in September 1986 and stayed there until his return to Nicaragua in August 1987. *La Prensa* was granted permission to reopen and begin publishing again in September 1987 and the first edition of the newspaper was published 1 October 1987.

Acknowledgements

THIS BOOK IS dedicated to the memory of Pedro Joaquín Chamorro Cardenal, whose example and values continue to crystallize both the meaning and the struggle of *La Prensa*. For the English revision, I want to gratefully acknowledge Dr. Alejandro Bolaños Geyer, the translator, and Steven Blakemore, the editor, for their assistance.

J.Ch.C.

Preface

WHEN I WAS a boy growing up in Granada, the flow of Nicaraguan history permeated the air we breathed, pulsating through the stones, the flowers, the very roots of our daily existence. Granada was the cradle of my ancestors, and we all celebrated our national heroes and their national wars against pirates, against the English, and finally against the North American filibuster William Walker. Was there a Nicaraguan who didn't know about the battle of San Jacinto and our heroes—General José Dolores Estrada, Andrés Castro, Emmanuel Mongalo, and the rest of the national ghosts who live today within our people?

This heritage of our national struggle against foreign intervention, including the intervention of the U.S. Marines, created a strong national mythos that is still a fundamental fact of Nicaraguan culture. The Chamorro family, and especially my older brother, Pedro Joaquín, luxuriated in this mythos. This is a fundamental point that most foreigners are unaware of, and it is pertinent for any understanding of Pedro Joaquín Chamorro Cardenal and his visceral aversion to hegemonic power in Nicaragua—whether this power is exercised by a colossus of the North or of the East. In Nicaragua today, we are experiencing a new kind of *filibusterismo*, a new kind of *Somocismo* magnified and perfected, for *Sandinismo* is essentially scientific *Somocismo*.

In writing a book about *La Prensa*, I write not merely of a financial enterprise, a business association—but of Nicaragua and its people and the newspaper through which they expressed themselves. I thus have an obligation to them as well as to restless ghosts resentful of foreign presences.

In the history of our Hispano-American culture, the institution that traditionally defends liberty and human rights is the press. Indeed, the press is the principal countervailing voice that directly confronts oppressive state power. In Central America, freedom of the press is the political, social, and cultural thermometer that measures and reveals the condition of the other attendant liberties that constitute a nation's health. Hence freedom of the press is inextricably intertwined with our people's freedom.

In this sense, *La Prensa* is and was all the people who suffered. Thousands suffered imprisonment or violence because they published their opinions in *La Prensa*. Likewise, *La Prensa* published and protested information about the oppression of the people by both the Somoza and Sandinista dictatorships, and its journalists were imprisoned and tortured by both. *La Prensa* denounced and protested: that is what gave the paper its popular strength, that is why *La Prensa* is rooted in the history of Nicaragua. The history of *La Prensa* is also the history and sacrifice of Pedro Joaquín Chamorro Cardenal, whose death detonated the revolution that destroyed the Somoza dictatorship.

Pedro and his fellow countrymen paid a high cost, but all the sacrifices, the sufferings, and the deaths crystallized a national unity around the revolution we were creating—uniting all the forces of that revolution and the body of principles for which multitudes of Nicaraguans died. With both his words and actions, Pedro created the national longing for a just, pluralistic, and republican revolution. In other words, it is precisely because the revolution was popularly understood as a revolution that would be both democratic and pluralistic that the entire country united in destroying the Somoza dictatorship.

In Nicaragua there was no ideological void as there was in Cuba. Here we had a system of beliefs sanctified by the blood of the dead; we had a body of principles created out of the collective endeavors of the Nicaraguan people. Consequently, we were all convinced that we were creating the first truly authentic revolution in Latin America: a revolution that was both social and political, a revolution that affirmed and defended both national honor and human dignity against any form of intervention, whether it be imperialist or totalitarian, domestic or foreign. And even when we saw the revolution betrayed, we still knew that this time it would be different—this time the revolution would return and reclaim itself.

The history of *La Prensa* is the history of a people's struggle against both the Somoza and Sandinista dictatorships. Threatened by the Somozas, Pedro Joaquín once said that "each person is the master of his own fear." How often during the past nine years we have had to relearn what these words mean. And what are nine years compared to forty-three years of the Somoza dictatorship? The major part of this book is devoted to Sandinista repression of *La Prensa*, but not because one dictatorship is "better" and we must choose. That is precisely the tragedy of Latin America— we have always been given just two choices: a dictatorship of the right or of the left. This is our historical false dilemma, the choice forced on us by both monsters. And how we have known both monsters—the boot in the face, the institutional repression, Somocista jails transformed into Sandinista prisons.

In Nicaragua, we have known both monsters intimately, for after they swallowed us and we saw their sterile souls through the bleak night of history, we saw that both monsters were astonishingly similar. Both monsters craved possession, one obsessed with an ideology of greed, the other with an ideology of power.

And so we refuse to choose and be tricked into saying one is "better," for we Nicaraguans intend to do something truly revolutionary and break forever the vicious circle of right- and left-wing tyrannies. If we linger over the Sandinista monster, it is simply because the facts speak for themselves: the Sandinistas accomplished in seven years what the Somozas could not do in forty-three: they had—at least for a time—silenced *La Prensa*. Thus we can authoritatively assert that we have lived inside this monster, we know its entrails.

In 1972, soon after an earthquake had destroyed much of Managua, Anastasio Somoza sneeringly said of *La Prensa* that "it's only a piece of paper." We proudly took Somoza's pejorative phrase and turned it into "the Republic of Paper," for that is precisely how we envisioned *La Prensa*: Only in *La Prensa* was there anything resembling a republic, where different ideas could be exchanged and respected, where there was a pluralistic forum for opposing voices. Both dictatorships hated this "piece of paper"; both attempted to destroy the Republic of Paper.

One newspaper frightened two dictatorships, for most state censorship is a form of state cowardice—a censorship that hides behind rationalizations of power to justify state oppression. Hence dictatorships fear voices other than their own; they fear the moment when indignant ghosts rise out of their graves and a people overthrows its oppressors. It does not happen suddenly. The Somozas heard only the monolithic echoes of their own voices for forty years. But time has a way of dealing with dictators. Out of its irrevocable flow, a revolution betrayed turns ineluctably against the betrayers.

JAIME CHAMORRO CARDENAL

LA PRENSA

From the Beginning through the Somozas

1.

FOR MANY YEARS, the Chamorro family has been associated with Nicaraguan history. Fruto Chamorro, my great-great uncle, was the first Nicaraguan president (1853-1855). He was followed by three other Chamorros who occupied the presidency during different epochs: Pedro Joaquín Chamorro (1875-1879), Emiliano Chamorro (1917-1921), Diego Manuel Chamorro (1921-1923), and Emiliano again briefly in 1926.

The Chamorro family has also been associated for many years with *La Prensa*—Nicaragua's principal independent newspaper. In its sixty-year history, *La Prensa* was subjected to multitudinous repressions and assaults by both the Somoza and Sandinista dictatorships, so in its own small way the history of *La Prensa* mirrors the contemporary history of Nicaragua.

La Prensa was founded by Pedro Belli, Gabry Rivas, and Enrique Belli on 2 March 1926. In 1929, José Maria Moncada, president of Nicaragua and head of the Liberal party, the principal political alternative to the Conservative party in Nicaragua, exiled Adolfo Ortega Díaz, *La Prensa's* editor in chief. Ortega Díaz died in exile. In 1930, my father, Pedro Joaquín Chamorro Zelaya, became editor in chief; and in 1932, he bought the paper with the intention of publishing historical studies about Nicaragua as well as promoting the principles of the Conservative party, of which he was an ardent member. During his presidency, Moncada briefly closed

La Prensa several times, and he revoked its right to send mail without charge within the country. In 1931, an earthquake leveled Managua, and *La Prensa*'s installations were also destroyed; a few months later, they were rebuilt.

In 1933, *La Prensa* was temporarily closed by the government of President Juan Bautista Sacasa for unspecified reasons. In 1934, *La Prensa* was closed for three days after Augusto C. Sandino, his brother Sócrates, and two of his generals were murdered on orders by Anastasio Somoza García, head of the National Guard. In its final days, the government of Sacasa closed *La Prensa* on 15 January 1935 for one day.

Thus, although there was a tradition of brief censorship and mild harassment of newspapers in Nicaragua, it did not reach the repressive, systematic levels perfected later by the Somoza and Sandinista dictatorships. In fact, freedom of the press was nominally respected and was guaranteed by all the Nicaraguan constitutions.

But all this began to change when Anastasio Somoza García overthrew Sacasa in a coup d'état in 1936. Somoza replaced Sacasa with an interim president, Carlos Brenes Jarquín, who then temporarily closed *La Prensa*. Somoza became president in 1936 and began a policy of periodic censorship and interminable threats against *La Prensa* for the remainder of the decade.

During the Second World War, Somoza increased and consolidated his power and, in order to silence criticisms of his personal greed, he created "blacklists" and decrees controlling the rationing of paper, ink, and printing supplies, thus exercising capricious and arbitrary control over the press.

Horacio Ruiz, a distinguished editor of *La Prensa*, remembers this period well: "I will always remember one afternoon when a National Guard officer entered the newspaper office and asked Dr. Pedro Joaquín Chamorro Zelaya to accompany him. Somoza was very angry about an article he had written. Don Pedro unaffectedly put on his white denim coat that was hanging on the back of a chair and bid farewell saying, 'Well, I guess I'll be back when I can,' and was then imprisoned in the *Casa de Piedra* [Stone House] at the *Campo de Marte*" ["Martial Field" military compound in Managua]. This happened in the early '40s. On another occasion, Somoza shut down *La Prensa* for three days when his wife, Salvadora Debayle, complained that her name had been omitted in the chronicle of a list of ladies at a party.

In 1945, Anastasio Somoza ordered a total shutdown of *La Prensa*.

Consequently, my father had to go into exile with his family. Somoza had intended to reelect himself as president, but an opposition campaign, in conjunction with public demonstrations by the 1944 generation of high school and university students and *La Prensa* editorials, thwarted his efforts, forcing him to impose Leonardo Argüello as candidate for the 1947 elections. *La Prensa* was reopened in 1946, after being forcibly closed for one year.

On 26 May 1947 Somoza overthrew Leonardo Argüello, whom he had placed in the presidency less than a month earlier. Somoza personally telephoned *La Prensa* the following day and shouted that those in *La Prensa* must stop publishing rubbish and that the newspaper was immediately suspended. The person who received the call thought that it was a prank and told Somoza (whose voice he did not recognize) to stop bothering him. Somoza shouted again, identifying himself and confirming that *La Prensa* was suspended.

In 1952, my father died and my older brother, Pedro Joaquín Chamorro Cardenal (coeditor since 1948) became the new editor of *La Prensa*, rapidly improving it. Pedro was born on 23 September 1924 in the city of Granada. He was always an individualist who distinguished himself in his various endeavors. From the beginning, he personally opposed the Somoza dynasty, seeing it as a fatal interruption in the flow of Nicaraguan history. In the 1940s, while he was a law student at the National University in Managua, he joined an anti-Somoza protest group. As a result of his antigovernment activities he was arrested and exiled to Mexico where he graduated with a law degree from the National Autonomous University of Mexico. After returning to Nicaragua in 1948, Pedro married Violeta Barrios in 1950.

On 22 May 1953 the mayor of Managua, General Andrés Murillo, sent Somocista mobs, accompanied by the armored support of a Caterpillar tractor, to assault *La Prensa*'s new two-story building. Fortunately, our workers surrounded the building, creating a human barrier, and the Somocistas withdrew. This incident greatly amused Somoza, and he referred to it as the *tractorazo* (the tractor "blow").

Beginning in April 1954, Somoza imposed strict prior censorship that lasted months, and he sent Pedro to a military court that subsequently sentenced and imprisoned him for taking part in a rebellion against the government. After being tortured, he was released early.

La Prensa's coeditor-in-chief, Pablo Antonio Cuadra, was also jailed along with many *La Prensa* journalists. Censorship was so prolonged and so intense that *La Prensa*'s staff had to make use of an Ava Gardner photo to fill in what the censor's red pencil had scratched out. The quick-witted newspaper boys began shouting in the streets of Managua: "*La Prensa*, with Ava Gardner!"—so everyone knew that *La Prensa* had been censored once again.

In 1956, Anastasio Somoza García was assassinated and succeeded by Luis Somoza Debayle, his oldest son and his dynastic successor. The Somozas accused Pedro of involvement in the assassination. *La Prensa* was militarily occupied, and Pedro Joaquín was once again jailed along with the entire *La Prensa* staff. While he was in prison, Pedro was tortured again and kept in leg irons. In addition, *La Prensa* was required to publish "condolences" and was then subjected to prolonged prior censorship.

During this time, Horacio Ruiz, head of the editorial staff, was tortured into "confessing" that Pedro Joaquín was involved in the assassination, but he subsequently denounced both the torture and the forced confession during a trial in a military court. While Ruiz was imprisoned, Anastasio Somoza Debayle, head of the National Guard, arrived to question him. When Ruiz complained that the guards had not given him any water to drink for a long time and asked Somoza to intercede, Somoza replied, "When *La Prensa* arrives in the evening it spoils my appetite." (It should be noted that in his will, Pedro Joaquín denied having any prior knowledge of Somoza García's assassination.) After a period of house arrest in 1956 and 1957, Pedro was banished and then escaped with his wife, Violeta, to Costa Rica, where he was granted asylum.

In 1959, Pedro went to Havana to seek arms from Fidel Castro, but no agreement was reached because each mistrusted the other. On 30 May, Pedro landed in the provinces of Boaco and Chontales with 120 armed men, including myself, to overthrow Luis Somoza. Pedro, however, was captured, tried, sentenced and in 1960, released early. *La Prensa* was again censored. In his *Diario de un Preso* (*A Prisoner's Diary*), Pedro writes: "Yesterday, at the trial, I managed to get an old issue of *La Prensa*, and I read it from beginning to end. It says innocuous things, obviously because the censor has applied against it a pencil much bigger and heavier than mine. His marks are seen on all the pages; the gaps left by the deletions of the zealous representative of the state are silently eloquent" (19 September 1959).

Somoza also used mobs to intimidate the opposition. In his book *Estirpe*

Sangrienta: Los Somoza (The Bloody Lineage: The Somozas), Pedro graphically narrates how they were used when he arrived with other prisoners at the Court:

> When the van arrived at *Campo de Marte* barracks (high stone walls crenelated with sentry boxes, machine guns on tripods, long sandy streets, and prefab steel structures), we saw the surrounding area filled with people who, upon learning of the presence of the prisoners, let out a loud and resonant scream: "Murderers!"
>
> And behind the cloud of dust raised by the vehicle, as in a cloudy echo of heterogeneous voices, were masses of men and women, dancing like savages over their victims, bearing placards and shouting in indescribable confusion: "Let's kill them! Kill their children! Burn their homes! Murderers! You won't get out of here alive!..."
>
> And then we got out of the van, midst the barely concealed sneers of the *Campo de Marte* officers, who delivered us to the frenzy of the mob paid by the Somozas to throw rocks and spit on us.
>
> Headed by a woman named Nicolasa Sevilla, these mobs were known as the *Nicolasa*. It was the old method discovered by Somoza García in 1944, when he hired a number of prostitutes and set them on the mothers and wives of the political prisoners of that time, who had joined a march in protest against Somoza....
>
> On the first day, as we left the *Campo de Marte* courtroom, the crowd paid by Somoza went wild again with hysteria. As we approached the van that would again take us to jail, a surge of people came between us and the vehicle. Showers of rocks came from a distance, and those of the rabble closest to us tried to hit us as often as possible with the sticks they had been provided. They spat on us again until the door closed and the van sheltered us under its steely metal cover. We left amid a fearful frenzy, and even in the distance we could hear the same shouts that had greeted us in the morning: "Murderers!...Bandits!...We'll burn your houses!"

Nicolasa Sevilla's final chapter was pure burlesque. She was jailed and then pardoned by the Sandinista state: upon leaving prison, she offered her services to the new regime.

But the history of *La Prensa* is more than its opposition to repugnant dictators. *La Prensa* was popularly known as the "Voice of the People." In its pages, people from all walks of life could ask for assistance, accuse government officials of specific abuses, and share information with the populace. In addition, we at *La Prensa* had a moral and social obligation to the Nicaraguan people, with whom we are linked in destiny; for it was through our readers that *La Prensa* lived, and the voice of the people lived in *La Prensa*.

In September 1963, *La Prensa* promoted the first literacy campaign in Nicaragua. In Nicaragua, September is a month of special symbolic meaning, for it was on 15 September 1821 that Central America became independent from Spain, and on 14 September 1856 that our forces defeated the army of filibuster William Walker in the corrals of the San Jacinto hacienda.

In order to teach a large, illiterate population to read and write, Pedro Joaquín decided to use *La Prensa*. With modest tools he was able to cause a nationwide sensation. *La Prensa* published 100,000 primers, divulged the full National Literacy Plan, and circulated the map of Nicaragua which was then mostly unknown to the Nicaraguan people. The primers were technically prepared according to the Laubach method, approved and distributed by UNESCO, the United Nations' world educational organization. They had thirty-two quarter pages with profuse illustrations and large characters, clearly and neatly printed so that pupil and teacher could easily see the syllables, words, and phrases. At the end, there was a map of our country—rivers, plains, mountains, lakes, shores, coasts. Nicaragua suddenly appeared before humble eyes.

The direct fruits of the Patriotic Literacy Campaign began to be seen early in 1964. But the government of Luis Somoza would not allow advances in literacy, especially as it was the work of *La Prensa*. Thus, in that year, the Patriotic Literacy Campaign's National Committee was dissolved on orders from the dynastic dictator.

But Pedro Joaquín and *La Prensa* urged the people to continue the struggle for literacy—imploring those who were literate to help their less fortunate brothers and sisters. In one *La Prensa* editorial, Pedro wrote the following: "To learn to read isn't difficult, nor is it difficult to teach it. When appropriate tools and guidelines are available, a little good will and effort suffice. It is enough for those who don't know, to love to know, and for those who do know, to love their neighbor. Those who know how to read have an obligation to teach those who don't know. We don't want this to be our plan, but everybody's plan."

The literacy program then began to reach all Nicaraguans by radio, the most popular medium in Nicaragua. In the humble hut, in the lost settlement, in the depths of the jungle, and in the solitude of the farm, the voice of the radio announcer filled the air with sound, calling and teaching "he who doesn't know." Naturally, the dictatorship feared this enlightenment and cancelled the program.

When the Sandinistas launched the National Literacy Campaign in 1980, with the support of the entire country, they made no reference to that first battle against ignorance. They did not mention the initial effort of *La Prensa* and Pedro Joaquín, because they did not want it known that *La Prensa* had launched the first literacy campaign in Nicaragua.

In the 1960s, we added *La Prensa Literaria*, a cultural supplement that usually appeared in the Sunday newspaper. Created by Pablo Antonio Cuadra, *La Prensa Literaria* was an open forum for the creative voices of Nicaragua: the poets, fiction writers, and essayists who contributed to an indigenous Nicaraguan culture. In the late 1960s and '70s, many people who would soon have prominent positions in the Sandinista government or who were strongly identified with the Sandinistas contributed to *La Prensa Literaria*, including Ernesto Cardenal, Sergio Ramírez, Gioconda Belli, Rosario Murillo, and Carlos Mejía Godoy.

Together Pedro Joaquín and Pablo Antonio Cuadra turned *La Prensa* from a Conservative party newspaper into a newspaper that was democratic, pluralistic, and nationalist. They crystallized a philosophy that would inform *La Prensa*: *La Prensa* would be a forum for the oppressed who could use *La Prensa* to air their grievances, and we would equally criticize government abuses of power, while suggesting changes and reforms. We would be democratic and pluralistic, associated with the values of the West. *La Prensa* would be open to all persuasions and political ideologies. In addition, we would employ a style of journalism characterized as "Socratic Journalism." We decided that since journalism could serve as a catalyst to reveal the reality of politics and culture, we would attempt to reach the essence of events through a journalism that encouraged dialogue and irony, just as Socrates sought truth through the dialectic of questioning and reasoning. We thus attempted to promote an authentic Nicaraguan culture, rooted in the lives, the values, and the beliefs of the Nicaraguan people. For years, Nicaraguans had recognized *La Prensa* as "the newspaper of the Nicaraguans" and "the voice of the people," and we worked to be worthy of those titles. We did not want a procrustean, ideological program; we labored to create our newspaper out of the substance of Nicaraguan reality. As with any newspaper, we were not always successful. In the fast-paced chaos of daily publishing, we sometimes deviated from our standards. Nevertheless these standards inspired our endeavors. For us, *La Prensa* was the palpable voice for those who had no voice.

2.

In the meantime, we continued opposing the Somozas and their efforts to run Nicaragua as if it were their personal farm.

On 23 January 1967, when Lorenzo Guerrero was president, placed there provisionally by Luis and Anastasio Somoza after the unexpected death of President René Schick, the National Guard militarily occupied *La Prensa* for ten days. The Guard looted our offices and printing establishment and violated our files. They did this because Pedro had helped organize a public demonstration by the opposition in downtown Managua to protest the electoral fraud that Anastasio Somoza Debayle and his cronies were planning, following the death of Somoza's brother, Luis. (The Somoza elections were so notorious that on 31 October 1974, one day before another election won by Somoza, *La Prensa* carried a headline that announced, "Candidates who won tomorrow's elections.") The demonstration had erupted into a gunfight between the opposition and the National Guard. Many people were killed or injured. Pedro Joaquín was jailed for forty-five days and then released. Three opposition radio stations were temporarily closed.

In the 1970s, a revolutionary group founded in 1961 as the Sandinista Front of National Liberation (FSLN) began to draw attention. They called themselves Sandinistas, after Augusto César Sandino, the Nicaraguan nationalist who had fought the U.S. Marines intervening in Nicaragua in the 1920s. Although they appropriated Sandino's name, they were essentially Marxist-Leninist. During the first decade of their existence, they had attempted to overthrow the Somoza dynasty but had always been unsuccessful. In 1967, they suffered their worst defeat on a mountain peak north of Matagalpa, known as Pancasán. Of the thirty-five members who had taken part in the military campaign, twenty were killed by Somoza's National Guard. At the end of 1967, there were only fifty active FSLN members.

In the 1970s, the correlation of forces began to change. Somoza's imperial will to power had caused widespread discontent throughout Nicaragua. As the Sandinistas began to gather support in the universities, schools, churches, and among the children of the middle class, they started robbing banks and attacking the National Guard. The more successful they were, the more repressive the Guard became, and the more the Sandinistas grew in popularity. For most of the Nicaraguan people, tired and frustrated with the Somoza dictatorship, the ubiquitous slogan was "anything's better than Somoza" (*"Mejor que Somoza cualquier cosa"*).

We at *La Prensa* were also sympathetic. As *La Prensa* was the principal symbol of opposition to the Somoza dynastic dictatorship, many Sandinistas and their sympathizers incorporated themselves into the newspaper. Among them were Bayardo Arce, Sergio Ramírez, and William Ramírez —subsequently important members in the Sandinista government. Tomás Borge had formerly been a *La Prensa* agent in León.* Rosario Murillo, who would become Daniel Ortega's common-law wife, was Pedro Joaquín's secretary for twelve years. Pedro Joaquín, himself, was suspected and despised by the Sandinistas as a member of the hated bourgeoisie, but because his popularity and opposition to Somoza benefited them, they were content to use Pedro and *La Prensa* for their own ends. Yet Pedro himself had no illusions about the Sandinistas. He knew that they were Marxist-Leninists, and he disliked how they had appropriated Sandino— one of his national heroes. He considered the Sandinistas to be young and misguided, but he characterized their war against Somoza as a struggle against an "illegitimate government." Thus, while there was no love between them, they shared an uneasy tactical understanding about the necessity of deposing Somoza.

On 23 December 1972 an earthquake destroyed most of Managua, including the offices of *La Prensa*. However, by March 1973 *La Prensa* was rebuilt at its present location on the North Highway, also known now as Pedro Joaquín Chamorro Road. After the earthquake, massive foreign aid had poured into Nicaragua, but Somoza and his cronies misappropriated much of it, leaving thousands of Nicaraguans destitute. In *La Prensa*, we accused Somoza of mismanaging the funds and documented how his cronies had also misused them.

In October 1973, after accusations in *La Prensa* that public officials were making fortunes, a law was passed subjecting newsmen to fines

---

* Among Borge's responsibilities was that of opening *La Prensa* agencies in the Western part of the country. In the town of Telica, he founded the *La Prensa* agency run by Santiago Torres. Recently Torres's widow was interrogated by Sandinista police and was asked who had convinced her to sell *La Prensa*. They were astonished when she replied, "Comandante Tomás Borge," explaining that he had founded the agency when he was a *La Prensa* employee in León. In 1956, after Borge was arrested following the assassination of Somoza García, *La Prensa* continued supporting his family.

for "defaming" government officials. Journalists throughout the hemisphere protested.

In December 1974, after a Sandinista commando unit burst into a reception at the home of a Somoza cabinet minister, José María Castillo, killing him and holding the guests hostage, Anastasio Somoza imposed strict censorship. Although the mediation of Archbishop Miguel Obando y Bravo, requested by the Sandinistas, put an end to the episode by an agreement on both sides, Somoza maintained the censorship against *La Prensa* until September 1977: almost three consecutive years of prior censorship, the longest period of censorship under the Somozas—today amply surpassed by Sandinista censorship. It should be pointed out that under Somoza, with one exception, the censors were from the military, and the Sandinistas have followed his example.

Somoza, of course, accused all of us in *La Prensa* of being Communists, and in 1975 his government press office released a white paper supposedly showing similarities between articles and editorials in *La Prensa* and various Sandinista proclamations. According to the government's logic, this proved that "the editor of *La Prensa* and the Sandinista terrorists are conspiring jointly."

On 9 June 1976 Judge Rosa Argentina Montenegro ordered *La Prensa* to pay C$75,000 (*córdobas*, then worth over $10,000), in an arbitrary sentence for matters concerning the paid ads section. In addition, Pedro Joaquín was required to pay a personal fine of C$25,000 (over $3,500), but he paid the fine in *córdoba* quarters, and Nicaraguans enjoyed his joke on Somoza. In 1977, Somoza lifted the rigid three-year period of censorship, and Pedro responded by running the previously censored material in subsequent *La Prensa* issues.

Between 1977 and 1979, Somoza either fined or temporarily closed five radio stations: *Radio Futura, Radio Mi Preferida, Radio Corporación, Radio Mundial,* and *Radio Fabuloso Siete*—radio stations that would soon become Sandinista targets as well.

During the last two years of Somoza's government, opposition forces joined in various alliances to intensify internal pressure. In conjunction with various external pressures—the OAS condemnation of the government, Mexico's diplomatic break in relations, the intervention of Venezuela and Costa Rica (the latter having become an open sieve for arms shipped from Cuba to Panama and then through Costa Rica to the Sandinistas), and the pressure coming from the Carter administration itself—this correlation of forces combined to number Somoza's days. We, at *La Prensa*, also intensified our attacks on Somoza, reporting openly on the government's deteriorating position. A characteristic example is the 10 September 1978 issue of *La Prensa*, which carried front-page news on simultaneous Sandinista attacks on different fronts as well as economic strikes carried out by the democratic opposition. All this accumulated pressure flowed from an event that finally destroyed the Somoza dictatorship.

On 10 January 1978, as Pedro was driving to work, a green Toyota suddenly blocked his way. Two men approached and fired three shotgun blasts through the driver's window. Pedro died later in an ambulance on his way to the hospital. Thousands of Nicaraguans took to the streets in explosive rioting. The national insurrection that would bring Somoza down had started.

After Pedro was murdered, *La Prensa* was turned into an opposition headquarters, and many of the Sandinistas in the newspaper formed secret Sandinista cells. In the newspaper, Pedro Joaquín's photo was carried on the front page every day with a call for justice. Some of the headlines for this period (10-23 January) included the following: "Hired Assassins," "The people know who the Assassin is," "It is time to clench fists," "Violeta: Somoza knows." Indeed, Pedro Joaquín's death ignited the national insurrection against Somoza—for everyone assumed Somoza was behind it. Hence people who had been neutral or indifferent aligned themselves with all the national forces opposing the dictatorship. It was as if his death released forty years of suppressed rage against the repression and humiliation buried in the Nicaraguan psyche.

Thus it is crucial to stress that the revolution that brought the Sandinistas to power was a national revolution in which all the people participated. The Sandinistas never had more than several hundred men in arms, but with Pedro Joaquín's death, the entire country joined the war against Somoza. Taking advantage of this strategic moment, the Sandinistas talked of a "third way," neither Communist nor Capitalist. They emphasized basic rights, freedoms and guarantees, and played down their Marxist-Leninist ideology.

In August 1978, my family loaned the Sandinistas $50,000 for an unspecified "revolutionary operation" that we believe culminated in the takeover of the National Palace by Edén Pastora and his commando team on 21 August 1978. We made the check, drawn from a Miami bank, to the wife of Ernesto Castillo, currently the Sandinistas' ambassador to the Soviet Union. Xavier Chamorro, who is currently editor of *El Nuevo Diario*, was the only family member who objected. When they were subsequently reminded of their pledge to repay the loan, the Sandinistas ignored us. It has never been paid back.

On 11 June 1979, a defeated Somoza, in one final furious attack against his old nemesis, ordered the National Guard to destroy *La Prensa*. Around 3:00 P.M., an armored vehicle fired at point-blank range and then some National Guardsmen climbed over our fence while others passed them cans of gasoline, which they then poured over the building. A Cessna then fired rockets at our newspaper offices. *La Prensa* was destroyed, but Somoza's victory was fleeting. He had destroyed a building, but the spirits of Pedro Joaquín and *La Prensa* were soon resurrected out of the ashes. The next day, as people fled the fighting in Managua, they waved white handkerchiefs in homage to a newspaper that had also been part of them. A little over a month later, Somoza fled the country, and the Sandinistas entered Managua on 19 July 1979.

We can close the Somoza era by considering repressive Somoza legislation and the characteristics of *Somocismo* as it affected press freedom in Nicaragua. In the long reign of the Somozas, three press laws governed the expression of written thought. The first was the 1953 Press Law that, under the pretext of "regulating" the constitutional right of unrestricted freedom of the press, in fact subjected press freedom to so many limitations that it almost destroyed it. However, a few newspapers (among them *La Prensa*), refused to comply with all its provisions and continuously protested its impositions.

The people appropriately baptized this law with the name "Gag Law," and on 10 October 1958 it had to be replaced by the "Law of Elucidations and Rectifications" that, in a more subtle way, also restricted the "unrestricted" freedom of the press proclaimed in the constitution of the republic of Nicaragua. The first law, or Gag Law, was issued under Anastasio Somoza García, and the second one, which the opposition called the "Yoke Law," was issued under his son, Luis Anastasio Somoza Debayle.

Another Press Law that fettered freedom of speech in a similar way was issued on 25 January 1967, when Anastasio Somoza Debayle became the last dynastic Somoza candidate. In April 1974, that law was replaced by the provisions of the new Penal Code which, taking advantage of its classification of Insults and Slanders (Chapter VII, Articles 169 to 194), threatened press freedom through a series of penalties: dollar fines and other pecuniary punishments, jail for the authors of the offense, including the directors, editors, and those who owned the printing press when the offense took place in a newspaper or anything that they printed. In all, *La Prensa* was either closed or censored nine times by the Somozas, for various periods of time.

Under the Somozas, freedom of the press was, at best, always precarious. But many journalists were able to defy the Somozas' anti-press legislation and eventually, with all Nicaragua turning against him, Somoza Debayle was forced, at times, to respect press freedom.

Except during the repeated "States of Siege," in which Martial Law suspended rights and guarantees and imposed prior censorship, the practice of journalism and the strengthening of certain press freedoms were heroic achievements, as demonstrated by our martyred editor, who sacrificed his life defending and practicing freedom of speech in *La Prensa*.

To crystallize the characteristics of censorship under the three Somozas (from Somoza García, the elder, to Anastasio Somoza Debayle), we quote again from Pedro Joaquín Chamorro Cardenal's testimony in his book *Estirpe Sangrienta: Los Somoza:*

> Somoza's journalistic enterprises enjoyed various privileges and prerogatives, while those of his enemies were persecuted to death. He stored his paper stock in public buildings, like the National Stadium, and through his friends he kept the other Managua newspaper reporters from obtaining news at official sources before the reporters of his own paper *(Novedades)*. His private business employees were on the government payroll; he paid their travel expenses outside the country (even to cover international sports events) with government funds. He repaired his machines in government shops; he forced government agencies to pay subscriptions and ads for his own benefit. In contrast, he jailed, obstructed, threatened, beat, and exiled those who attacked his system of government. And once he ordered his men to place chains around the printing press of a newspaper in a province.

The Sandinistas in Power 1979-1980

WHILE THE COUNTRY was celebrating the fall of Somoza, we were also busy rebuilding *La Prensa*. With international help, *La Prensa* reappeared on 16 August, twenty-seven days after the triumph of the national insurrection to which it had contributed. In this new stage, it was printed at *El Centroamericano* press, in León, eighty-five kilometers from Managua; *El Centroamericano* had ceased publication and its owner rented the press to print *La Prensa*.

Even before the ashes had cooled, spontaneous and generous offers from foundations and international organizations for *La Prensa's* reconstruction had arrived, and the Inter-American Press Association (IAPA) sent several pieces of equipment donated by its members.

The Friedrich Naumann Foundation, a foundation affiliated with the Free Democratic Party (FDP) of West Germany, sent us an agent who understood what had to be done to restore the physical plant, to reconstruct the offset press, and to finance new photocomposition and photomechanical equipment. Towards that end, he granted us a loan of $545,000 for the term of ten years, with a one-year grace period, at 2 percent annual interest, to be repaid in *córdobas*. The project was immediately implemented with a simple contract, without bureaucratic red tape or unnecessary paperwork, and thus, by mid-1980, with our plant in full operation, we moved from León to Managua.

In contrast, the Sandinista regime did not help at all, despite the fact that we had provided technical assistance in the transformation of Somoza's old daily, *Novedades*, into *Barricada*, the official newspaper of the FSLN. They only granted us an exemption of custom duties for the importation of the used equipment sent by the Inter-American Press Association (IAPA), of which we were members.

During this time, the Sandinistas soon revealed their plans for the remaining independent media in Nicaragua: They issued repressive legislation. Thus it is important to note that the Sandinistas had mandated and enforced repressive legislation from the very beginning—especially through a series of laws and ordinances which made freedom of expression contingent upon a range of deliberately ambiguous criteria—and established prior censorship for whatever the Sandinistas arbitrarily decided were economic and national security matters. Indeed, the Sandinista state has promulgated so many repressive laws that all of Somoza's juridical resources would today be treated with indifference, now that there exist the *Law to Regulate Information about National Security* (Decree #511), the *Law to Regulate Economic Information* (Decree #512), and the *General Provisional Law on Communications Media* (Decree #48), and its reform and subsequent implementation (Decree #708).

But this was just the beginning. From the Sandinista triumph of 19 July 1979, until March 1986 (when we began to compile data for this book), the Sandinista state had promulgated 1,732 decrees and laws: an average of five decrees per week. The Sandinistas, of course, initially promised that things would be different under them. They promised a free press.

On 18 June 1979, the Government Junta issued its first proclamation from "somewhere in Nicaragua." Point #14 deals with, among other things, "the free emission of information and diffusion of thought...all laws that repress the free emission and diffusion of thought and liberty of information are abolished."

On 20 July 1979, the Sandinistas issued the *Fundamental Statute of the Republic* (sanctioned 21 August by means of Decree #52) which contains the *Statute on the Rights and Guarantees of the Nicaraguan People*. Article #21 of *The Rights* guarantees free expression for everyone, and this includes "the liberty to seek, to receive, and to disseminate information and ideas, whether oral or written or by printing or in the form of art— or by whatever other mode of choice." But all this was for international consumption.

For at the same time (20 July) that the Sandinistas were abolishing all repressive Somocista legislation through Decree #8, *Abolishment of Repressive Laws* (in *La Gaceta*, no. 2, 23 August 1979), they simultaneously put into effect their own repressive legislation. For instance, on 22 July, they dictated Decree #10, the *Law of National Emergency* (in *La Gaceta*, no. 1, 22 August 1979)—which placed all media under government control "in the form that the government determines." Note that this decree appeared prior to Decree #8 in *La Gaceta*, the official record for Nicaraguan laws.

On 16 August 1979, less than a month after the Sandinista triumph, the Junta issued the *General Provisional Law on Communications Media* (Decree #48) in which freedom of expression is made conditional "within the real exercise of social responsibility." Indeed, the media should "offer true news inside a coherent context, acting as a correct reflection of the social groups and correctly valuing and strengthening the common objectives of the collective community." This opaque prose, a mixture of coercive ideology and bureaucratic pretentiousness, allows the government to determine what "true news" is. The *General Law* adds that all criticism of public functions "should express a legitimate preoccupation for the defense of the revolution's conquests, the process of reconstruction, and the problems of the Nicaraguan people—the media should not be instruments of antipopular interests."

This vague prose can, again, be interpreted any way the Sandinistas please. Indeed, it conditions free expression, "criticism," and "antipopular interests" within a vague Sandinista context. Thus it could be converted into a catchall to prevent anything the Sandinistas decide is antisocial criticism in the service of "antipopular interests."

The *General Law* went into effect 27 September, and article #42 gave the General Coordinator of the Division of Media and Communications the power "to order the suspension of every kind of publication, movies, or TV and radio transmissions in cases contemplated in article #3 of the *Media Law* and its nine clauses dealing with unacceptable materials." This ordinance was signed by Ernesto Cardenal, minister of culture, and authorized suspensions for forty-eight hours or longer or permanent suspensions for repeated violations.

The Ministry of Interior, headed by Tomás Borge, soon assumed the general coordinator's functions. On 10 September 1980, the Sandinistas issued Decrees # 511 and # 512, establishing prior censorship for matters of national security. Decree #511 contains the *Law to Regulate Information on Internal Security and National Defense* and stipulates that the Nicaraguan media cannot divulge news or information that compromises internal security or national defense. Decree #512 contains the *Law to Regulate Economic Information* and prohibits the release of news or information referring to the scarcity of products for popular consumption or any information that may lead to price speculation. Thus the government could again determine what constitutes security, defense, and economic information. In short, between August 1979 and September 1980 alone, repressive Sandinista legislation was mandated and enforced before the Contras had given the Sandinistas the pretext to continue doing what they had done all along.

Because of *La Prensa*'s national and international prominence, the Sandinistas, at first, went after the other independent media. It is important to focus on this briefly, because the fate of any independent newspaper is inextricably intertwined with the fate of all the independent media. The fact that even one can be censored, closed, or destroyed has ominous implications for the rest. In fact, as soon as they took over, the Sandinistas began systematically eliminating the other independent media.

There are two television stations in Nicaragua. In 1979, the Sandinistas confiscated one and gained control of the other through a combination of blandishments and threats. Both were then incorporated into the Sandinista Television System (SSTV). The confiscated station belonged to Somoza and carried two channels; the other station was independently owned by Sacasa Raskowsky and Company and carried four channels—three of them were *repetidoras*: satellite channels that carried the programming of the main channel into different parts of the country. The Sacasa-Raskowsky station was not Somocista, even though it has been misrepresented as such. The news anchorman for its principal channel was Manuel Espinoza Enríquez, who daily criticized the Somoza regime in his broadcasts. In 1979, the Sandinistas appointed Espinoza press secretary for the Junta, and today he is press secretary for the presidency. The Sandinistas have not allowed anyone to obtain an independent TV station.

In December 1979, Fabio Gadea, a Somoza opponent and the independent owner of three radio stations, applied for a permit to open a new independent TV station. Daniel Ortega denied the request and, in a televised speech, declared that television in Nicaragua would belong to the "people" and not to the "millionaires of the bourgeoisie." Ortega did not mention that under Sandinista law, any Nicaraguan citizen could apply for a license to operate radio or TV stations.

At the same time they were confiscating Somoza's TV station, the Sandinistas also confiscated a Somoza tabloid, *La Prensa Grafica*, and Somoza's newspaper, *Novedades*, converting the latter into *Barricada*, the official newspaper of the FSLN. *El Nuevo Diario*, the other state-subsidized paper, was created in April 1980.

In January 1980, the Sandinistas stormed the headquarters of the ultra-left newspaper, *El Pueblo*, jailing its editor and putting it out of business. On this occasion, I insisted that we publish an editorial in *La Prensa* protesting the government's action, but I was overruled by my brother, Xavier Chamorro, and Danilo Aguirre, respectively acting editor and news editor of *La Prensa*. Both of them argued that it would be inconvenient to defend *El Pueblo* because it was promoting "anarchy and chaos." Bayardo Arce, one of the nine comandantes on the National Directorate, declared that "the same medicine would be applied" to any newspaper or radio station that was not consistently sympathetic to the revolution. Until *La Prensa* resumed publication on 1 October 1987 (after being closed on 26 June 1986), there was not one independent newspaper in Nicaragua and, with the exception of a few scarcely read tabloids like the Communist party's *Avance*, all the other principal newspapers were Sandinista-controlled. *(Avance* was closed for three months in early 1985 after suggesting that the 1984 elections were fraudulent.)

Radio is the most important form of media in Nicaragua: many more people listen to radio than read newspapers or watch television. In July 1979, there were eighty-three radio stations and one state station, *Radio Nacional*. The Sandinistas converted the latter into *La Voz de Nicaragua*— the official radio station of the Sandinista government. Another station, *Estación Equis*, was owned by Somoza and was consequently confiscated and converted by the Sandinistas into *Radio Sandino*, the official station of the FSLN. In addition, the Sandinistas officially confiscated thirteen other stations that were either owned by Somoza or in some way associated with him. The Sandinistas also unofficially confiscated many of the lesser-known stations located in the provinces.

In 1980, practically no one objected to the confiscation of the Somoza media. But with control of the only two TV stations, two out of three newspapers, and at least fifteen out of eighty-three radio stations, the Sandinistas already had a hegemonic monopoly of the communications media.

In January 1980, the government ordered the suspension of a radio program directed by Oscar L. Montalvan, a journalist who had been a vigorous opponent of the Somoza dictatorship. In April 1980, a radio newsman, Guillermo Treminio, was arrested and sentenced to eleven months' imprisonment for supposedly broadcasting information "detrimental to the revolution." By September 1980, the Sandinistas had already issued Decrees # 511 and # 512, which made freedom of expression contingent upon a range of deliberately ambiguous criteria, and had established prior censorship for whatever the Sandinistas arbitrarily decided were economic and national security matters.

On 13 February 1981, Fabio Gadea, an outspoken opponent of Somoza and the owner of the largest independent radio station, and his wife were beaten by a Sandinista mob. Gadea later went into exile. On the night of 14 March 1981, a veritable night of terror, *Radio Corporación, Radio Mundial, Radio Mi Preferida,* and *Radio Amor* were surrounded by Sandinista mobs and threatened, as were *Radio Católica* and *Radio Tiempo*. These radio stations had been broadcasting news about the political meeting of the popular Nicaraguan Democratic Movement (MDN), headed by Alfonso Robelo, a former member of the Sandinista Junta, that was to take place the next day. *Radio Amor* and *Radio Mi Preferida* were partially destroyed by the mobs and later closed by the government.

In July 1981, the Sandinistas prohibited Archbishop Obando y Bravo's Mass to be televised, even though it had been televised for several years. In March 1982, *Radio Católica*, the Church's broadcasting station, was closed down for a month on the grounds that it had broadcast "inaccurate information" regarding a mob takeover of a church. In April 1983, the government announced that all sermons had to be submitted to the Ministry of Interior for prior censorship before they could be broadcast. Live broadcasts were prohibited and passages from the Bible were also censored.

On 17 January 1982, Manuel Jiron, owner of two confiscated radio stations, was attacked and beaten by three gunmen who attempted to kidnap him. Jiron received a head wound that required fourteen stitches. He had to go into exile.

Between January and February 1982, a government media censor, Vilma Auxiliadora Reyes, indefinitely suspended nine news programs and permanently closed two radio stations. Although some of the programs briefly returned after a couple of weeks, all were again suspended indefinitely in March.

On 15 March 1982, the government declared a state of emergency and closed down all the independent news programs broadcast on seven independent radio stations. In all, twenty-four news programs were suspended:

Radio Corporación: "6 de la Mañana," "Noticiero de las 11," "5 en Punto," "10 en Punto," and "Resumen de Noticias."

Radio Mundial: "Noticiero Mundial," "Hoy," "La Verdad," and "Actualidad Informativa."

Radio Mil: "IV Poder," "La Opinión," "La Opinión Científica," "Noticiero Mil."

Radio Católica: "Noticiero Adelante," "Noticiero Ya," "Noticiero Prensa Libre," "La Nación," "Diario de Hoy," "Noticias y Comentarios."

Radio Fabulosa 7: "El Día," "Noticias del 7," "Noticiero 5 PM."

Radio 590: "El Planeta."

Radio San Cristóbal: "Noticiero San Cristóbal y Darío."

Of the seven independent stations, *Radio Corporación* and *Radio Mil* were *intervenidas*, meaning that while legal ownership technically stayed with the owners, the government, in effect, controlled the stations.

In addition to the series of restrictions stringently applied to the media, the new Sandinista censor, Nelba Cecilia Blandón, issued her own decree ordering all radio stations to hook up every six hours with the government's radio station, *La Voz de Nicaragua*, in order to broadcast the Sandinista news program "La Voz de la Defensa de la Patria" ("The Voice of the Country's Defense"). Moreover, she required all media, both written and broadcast, to submit their daily programs or editorial copy to her office for prior censorship.

Within three months after the state of emergency had been imposed, many Nicaraguans began turning to foreign news stations for alternative news and information. Consequently, the government allowed a few of the suspended news programs to broadcast again, albeit under prior censorship. In October 1983, the government confiscated a transmitter from independent *Radio Mundial* and closed the station for a time, alleging that its license was out of order.

By 1983, 62 percent of all radio stations were controlled by the Sandinistas, and all were under prior censorship. Seventy-five percent of the radio news programs were Sandinista party programs. Of the suspended news programs, six were subsequently reinstated, but five of the six are today broadcast over Sandinista stations—the sixth is broadcast by the privately owned *Radio Mundial*. All of the news commentators appear to be Sandinista supporters. The six programs, each of them one hour in length, are listened to by hundreds of thousands of people, even though they operate under censorship and must observe restrictions set by the government. All the nominally independent stations have been intimidated into following the Sandinista party line or broadcasting music and other innocuous programming.

In addition to confiscating or destroying radio stations, the Sandinistas have imprisoned and mistreated various broadcast journalists, especially Nicaraguans associated with *Radio Impacto*, a popular Costa Rican radio station accused by the government of being counterrevolutionary. On 28 April 1984, Luis Manuel Mora Sanchez was arrested by Sandinista Security in Managua and sentenced to nine years in prison by the notorious anti-Somocista Tribunals. Mora, who also worked for *La Prensa*, was imprisoned the first time—he was to be imprisoned four times—for broadcasting interviews with mothers whose sons had been drafted under the mandatory military service law instituted by the government in 1983. He was subjected to psychological and physical torture. He was beaten, kept naked, handcuffed to the wall of his cell, deprived of food and water, and taken to cells that were alternately cold and hot, under conditions that he later characterized as "inhuman." He was also forced to "confess" that he had conspired against the revolution along with well-known politicians, members of the Catholic hierarchy (including Archbishop Obando), and the leaders of the two independent labor unions. He was pardoned in September and released.

On 22 December 1984, Salomón Calvo Arrieta, another Nicaraguan correspondent for *Radio Impacto*, was arrested by Sandinista Security and accused of transmitting information that "distorted reality." Calvo was also predictably accused of having links with the Contras and the CIA. He also happened to be a lawyer who had defended other Nicaraguans, including Mora Sanchez, before the anti-Somocista Tribunals. In addition, he was accused of distributing "tendentious" news about Jose Manuel Urbina Lara, a Nicaraguan suspected by the government of belonging to the Contras, who had taken refuge in the Costa Rican embassy six months before and who was forcibly removed by Sandinista Security forces on 24 December 1984. Calvo's wife, who had been present when he was arrested, declared that the Sandinistas first handcuffed and then beat him. He was released in February 1985 due to international pressure.

On 12 October 1985, the government confiscated the Catholic church's printing press and the first issue (10,000 copies) of its new magazine, *Iglesia*. The magazine remains banned. At the same time, the magazine for the Confederation for Labor Unity (CUS), an independent labor union, was closed by the government. According to the government, the magazine, *Solidaridad*, was closed because the government didn't "have enough censors" to read and check its contents. In addition, other banned publications include the bulletin of the Center of Nicaragua Workers (CTN);

the publication of the private business council COSEP, ¿Cómo Vamos?; the publication of the Independent Liberal Party, Paso a Paso; the monthly bulletin for the Democratic Conservative Party, En Marcha; and an independent newsletter called Prisma. (There are unconfirmed reports that Solidaridad and Pasa a Paso were subsequently allowed to be republished in January 1987.)

On 15 October 1985, the Sandinistas broadened the 1982 state of emergency and suspended a whole range of civil rights. Among the many restrictions was a regulation that required any organization outside the government to first submit any statement it wanted made public to the censorship bureau. Prior censorship for all Nicaraguan media had, of course, been in effect since March 1982.

In November 1985, the Permanent Human Rights Commission (CPDH), the only independent human rights organization in Nicaragua, was ordered to submit its monthly human rights reports to the government for prior censorship. Its director, Lino Hernández, was threatened with imprisonment if he disobeyed and continued to circulate the reports to foreign embassies and journalists.

On 25 November 1985, the Democratic Conservative Party denounced the closing of one of its radio programs by the Ministry of Interior. The program, "Conservatismo en Marcha," had broadcast complaints against the government's mandatory military service.

On 1 January 1986, the Sandinistas closed *Radio Católica* for inadvertently failing to join a required national radio hookup that broadcast a year-end message by President Daniel Ortega. In conjunction with the forced closing of *La Prensa* on 26 June 1986, the suspension of *Radio Católica* effectively eliminated the remaining independent media. [*Radio Católica* was reopened 2 October 1987.]

In May 1986, the government suspended "Deportivas Mundial" (World Sports), a sports program run by Mario Díaz on *Radio Mundial*. Díaz had violated a Sandinista taboo when he reported on Alexis Argüello, the Nicaraguan world boxing champion who was in exile and who supported the Contras.

On 4 May 1988, the government closed *Radio Corporación* for one day and suspended news programs carried by three other stations for eight days. They had all been reporting on a hunger strike by various groups of workers.

On 2 June 1988, the government suspended for ten days two news programs broadcast by *Radio Católica*. Both had transmitted a message from the Nicaraguan resistance contradicting government news about a Contra "deserter." The government hence continued violating the accords signed in Guatemala 7 August 1987 and in Sapoá on 23 March 1988, guaranteeing unrestricted press freedom.

On 6 June 1988 the government suspended the news program "Diez en Punto" for eight days. Broadcast by *Radio Corporación,* "Diez en Punto" was accused of reproducing "false information" transmitted by an international news agency.

On 11 July 1988, the government closed indefinitely *Radio Católica* for reporting on a violent Sandinista police attack on an opposition rally.

On 16 July 1988, the government closed indefinitely the popular news radio program *"El Despertar"* for broadcasting "false information."

Sandinista repression of the media did not begin or end with *La Prensa.* Once they took power and confiscated the Somocista media, the Sandinistas began the slow but inexorable silencing of the independent media. Today there is but one independent voice that can speak out or protest about what continues to happen in Nicaragua.

The Sandinistas were, however, initially more cautious in their campaign against *La Prensa*, essentially because our opposition to Somoza was indelibly on record both nationally and internationally. Thus, despite the fact that Comandante Daniel Ortega had already told one of our reporters in the first days of the Sandinista triumph that "newspapers like *La Prensa* should disappear," there was a series of friendly talks and visits with the Sandinistas, including one meeting which took place at the home of my brother, Xavier, the third of the Chamorro brothers and acting editor of *La Prensa.* Present at the meeting were Daniel Ortega and his companion Rosario Murillo, who had been our elder brother Pedro Joaquín's secretary at *La Prensa* for twelve years.

Both Ortega and his companion explained to us what "revolutionary journalism" should be and were candid about the kind of newspaper they wanted in Nicaragua. So we were not too surprised when, soon after that, while everyone in Nicaragua was still euphoric over the triumph of the revolution, the Sandinistas started referring to *La Prensa* as "the traitor newspaper," for certain minimal criticisms we had made of the new regime. Nor were we surprised when they began trying to gain control of the paper themselves. Before doing so, however, they had to get rid of the old management.

As a step in this direction, they offered to appoint *La Prensa*'s editor in chief, Pablo Antonio Cuadra, ambassador to Spain, and to appoint me, at that time general manager, ambassador to Argentina, Chile, and Uruguay (with residence in Buenos Aires), thereby getting us both conveniently out of the country. This would have left the paper in the hands of Xavier Chamorro, who had suddenly discovered the benefits of *Sandinismo*. But we turned down the Sandinistas' gambit.

Thus the Sandinistas focused their energies on trying to subvert *La Prensa* from within. As we still had many Sandinista sympathizers working for us, there was internal censorship imposed on articles suggesting even the mildest criticisms of the new government, especially on the editorial page. This led to a clash between Pedro Joaquín Chamorro Barrios, Pedro Joaquín's oldest son, and Danilo Aguirre, *La Prensa*'s news editor and the Sandinistas' primary agent within *La Prensa*. Xavier (who worked on the technical aspects of the paper) supported Danilo Aguirre, who received orders directly from Bayardo Arce, who had also worked for *La Prensa* and who was one of the nine comandantes. Aguirre also controlled *La Prensa*'s Sandinista Union, which then had a virtual veto power over articles on the editorial page.

On 27 February, Xavier Chamorro sent editor Horacio Ruiz an admonition on how to cover events relating to Cuba and the Soviet Union:

MEMORANDUM
TO: HORACIO RUIZ
FROM: THE MANAGING EDITOR
TOPIC: INTERNATIONAL NEWS
DATE: FEBRUARY 27, 1980.

On repeated occasions I have noticed the exaggerated way in which news about Cuba and the USSR are made to stand out in the headlines, as if we wished to convey an unfavorable image of those countries, the former of which has been giving extremely valuable aid to Nicaragua.

Therefore, it is necessary that just treatment be given to the Cuban affairs. For example, I don't consider it news for Nicaragua that thirty Cubans leave for Miami, or that a magazine exaggerates the Cuban problems that Fidel Castro himself has explained in his speeches, without concealing the economic problems that they have and that they are solving with adequate measures.

In reference to the USSR, it is necessary to use names correctly, for not only the Russians are Soviets, since Russia is merely one of the union formed by the Union of Soviet Socialist Republics.

Likewise, we must not emphasize news with sexual connotations, such as crimes, etc., not only because they are specifically forbidden by our Press Law, but also because of the most elementary ethics.
Having nothing else to relate,
XAVIER CHAMORRO CARDENAL
MANAGING EDITOR
YEAR OF THE LITERACY CAMPAIGN!
cc:Files.
XCHC/rmQuant.

Pedro Joaquín objected to this internal censorship and the loss of what he believed was *La Prensa*'s independence to criticize the abuses of the government. He was still, however, prevented from publishing articles critical of the government on various occasions, and even when he was occasionally permitted to publish something mildly critical, Xavier insisted that he do it anonymously. Posthumous *La Prensa* articles written by his murdered father were also prohibited. In addition, Pedro Joaquín was incensed that Aguirre ordered the composing room to add *coletillas,* or dissenting footnotes, a kind of political comment either disavowing or disagreeing with an article or editorial critical of the government or a story with a foreign dateline from a Western news agency—a tactic copied from Castro's Cuba in the first year of the Cuban revolution.

The all-family board of directors was increasingly concerned that Xavier was not independent enough and that, consequently, we were losing credibility with the people who were questioning our docility. Xavier, in turn, would insist that we must maintain a position of "critical support" for the revolution, by which he meant that we would support the revolution while offering "constructive" criticism. But Xavier never offered any criticism at all, and he continued to sanction the internal censorship.

La Prensa's all-family board of directors included Violeta Chamorro, the widow of our murdered editor, Pedro Joaquín Chamorro Barrios, Xavier Chamorro, Carlos Holmann and his wife Anita, and Margarita Cardenal de Chamorro, the mother of the three Chamorro brothers. When we had finally decided that Xavier had, in effect, aligned himself with the Sandinistas, he offered to resign several times. In the middle of April 1980, we accepted his resignation, although it was not written but pledged to us on his word of honor.

In the meantime, Violeta Chamorro, who was also one of the five members of the Sandinista Governing Junta, had resolutely decided to resign from the Junta (she had tried to resign twice before). The public reason given was that she had a broken foot, but the real reason was she could no longer support the Sandinistas' hegemonic tendencies: they had just illegally changed the composition of the Council of State, the principal legislative body in Sandinista Nicaragua. The Sandinistas had, in effect, "packed" the Council of State to favor themselves. And as they knew that Xavier had resigned and were concerned that this along with Violeta's impending resignation would create a crisis, several of the comandantes went to Xavier's house and asked him to delay things. The pertinent point is that they, in effect, asked him to forcibly resist the forthcoming change and retract his resignation.

On 19 April 1980, Alfonso Robelo, the only other democratic member of the Junta, who would soon resign for the same reasons Violeta did, called her to say that her resignation had been accepted and, for that purpose, the Governing Junta would be visiting her at her home.

Violeta vividly remembers that visit:

I was without a cook, and I decided to prepare a light lunch for them and my entire family, so that we would part on good terms. I ordered a paella [dish of rice with meat, chicken, fish, etc.] for twenty-five persons from a Spanish restaurant and called everyone who was invited. At 12:00 noon, on the dot, Tomás Borge was the first to arrive, with a large military retinue; the other comandantes and the Junta members, Moisés Hassán and Sergio Ramírez, came in later, one at a time. Daniel Ortega was last to arrive. Tomás then said that we should start the proceedings; but I told him that I would wait for Alfonso Robelo, who was away on some errand. The TV and radio journalists' equipment was already installed; I later asked them for the cassettes, but they never gave them to me.

Finally, Alfonso returned and the speeches began, and during the speeches of appreciation, I recall a child declaring that in the future he no longer would have to sell chewing gum, because chewing gum is imperialist. Afterwards I told him: "My son, there is nothing wrong with selling chewing gum if you do it honestly, because it is a job by which you earn your living, like any other." When the speeches ended the noise was awful; it was already 1:30 P.M. I approached one of the comandantes and told him I was planning on a light lunch, but I didn't have enough food for so many people. The others were ordered to leave, and only my family, the comandantes, and the Junta remained. Carlos Núñez sat next to me, and I told him: "Look, Carlos, I'm very worried." "But why?" said he, "We hold you in high esteem." "*Muchacho*," I replied, "I have a feeling that something bad may happen to me, that I may be thrown in jail, or may be killed, or who knows what." And shortly afterwards, at 3:00 P.M., they all left.

Doña Violeta's foreboding was justified, albeit in a different sense. On 20 April, I telephoned *La Prensa*'s composing room with instructions to save front-page space for an important announcement (Xavier's resignation) but *La Prensa*'s Sandinista supporters, who had been alerted beforehand, walked off the job, demanding that Xavier be retained as editor. We found out later that the walkout had been orchestrated by the Sandinistas through Danilo Aguirre. The order came directly from the Sandinista comandantes; it was an operation to take over *La Prensa* from within and was subsequently known as "Operation Trojan Horse."

In the meantime, the work stoppage had shut down *La Prensa*, and Xavier Chamorro and the Sandinista employees physically occupied the newspaper plant, taking control of the newspaper site. When, after all this, *La Prensa*'s board of directors still refused to give in, the Sandinistas sent an emissary to the home of two members of the board, Carlos Holmann and his wife Ana Maria, with an ultimatum from Bayardo Arce. If the board did not consent to the Sandinista proposals, the National Directorate would confiscate not only *La Prensa* but everyone's personal property as well. The Holmanns indignantly stood up and asked the emissary to leave.

By the end of April, the pressure had intensified, and the Sandinistas summoned *La Prensa*'s directors to a meeting with three comandantes: Bayardo Arce, Carlos Núñez, and Humberto Ortega. The comandantes insisted that the only person acceptable to them as editor of *La Prensa* —the only one they considered *consecuente* (sympathetic and understanding)—was Xavier Chamorro. They stated further that although we did not realize it, we were being used by the CIA to injure the revolution. After a few more exchanges along these lines, I finally told Bayardo Arce that as long as *La Prensa* still belonged to its legitimate owners we would go on acting as its directors. If the Sandinistas wanted it otherwise, they would have to confiscate the paper and put their own names on the masthead. The comandantes, having expected a different response, were surprised and confused.

In the end, a compromise was worked out. We gave Xavier 25 percent of our capital and the paper to start a new Sandinista newspaper called *El Nuevo Diario*. (Xavier had also wanted the exclusive use of the *La Prensa* motto, "The Newspaper of the Nicaraguans," but we refused to let him appropriate it.) In addition, he took with him 70 percent of *La Prensa*'s employees. Because of this, the Sandinistas claimed that *El Nuevo Diario* was the genuine *La Prensa* of old, claiming that a majority of *La Prensa*'s reporters and staff had gone over to *El Nuevo Diario*. But the latter was a deceptive half truth. First, some Sandinistas and their sympathizers had incorporated themselves into *La Prensa* during the insurrection against Somoza. Naturally, these would go to *El Nuevo Diario*. Moreover, many others went to *El Nuevo Diario* thinking *La Prensa* would be definitively closed: the government was making precisely this point through the state-controlled media, as was Danilo Aguirre. Thus many people, thinking of their futures, went to *El Nuevo Diario* believing that there would be no employment at *La Prensa*. When it became clear that *La Prensa* would not be closed, many of them returned asking for employment again, even though it was understood that once they left *La Prensa* they would never be reemployed.

Second, most of those who went over to *El Nuevo Diario* were from the technical and mechanical side of *La Prensa*: the majority of the primary staff remained with us: 60 percent of the editors, 70 percent of the managers, and 40 percent of the reporters. In addition, some of those who went to *El Nuevo Diario* were relatively new employees, while those who stayed were old *La Prensa* employees, such as Pablo Antonio Cuadra, Horacio Ruiz, Rafael Bonilla, Guillermo Ortega, Carlos Ramírez, Edgard Castillo, Octavio Escobar, and other *La Prensa* employees who had been with *La Prensa* and its assassinated editor, Pedro Joaquín Chamorro Cardenal, from the beginning. They represented both the old *La Prensa* and the independent line of Pedro Joaquín.

Finally, the Nicaraguan people have never recognized *El Nuevo Diario* as either the "old" or "new" *La Prensa*. Of the principal newspapers, it has always had the lowest circulation. Thus on 26 May 1980, thirty-five days after the attempted takeover, *La Prensa* resumed publication, quickly doubling its circulation and becoming, once again, Nicaragua's leading newspaper.

In early October 1980, the Sandinistas censored *La Prensa* for the first time after the Miskito Indians began protesting (in late September) the Cuban presence in Bluefields. This was the first massive antigovernment protest. On 1 October, we had reported on the protest, but the next day Manuel Espinoza Enríquez, the press secretary of the Governing Junta, invoked Decree #511 and prohibited *La Prensa* from publishing any information from Bluefields because of "national security." From that point on, *La Prensa* was forbidden to send any reporters to the Atlantic Coast. This was at a critical period during which the Sandinistas were just beginning to oppress the Miskito Indians.

On 8 November 1980, *La Prensa* protested the government's invocation of Decree #511 which prohibited "for reasons of national security" information about a meeting of the popular Nicaraguan Democratic Movement (MDN) in Nandaime. The meeting was cancelled by the government. The MDN was led by Alfonso Robelo, the former Junta member who had resigned after the Sandinistas had illegally changed the composition of the Council of State so that it was packed with a Sandinista majority. As Robelo and the MDN were extremely popular, the Sandinistas considered them a threat to their rule. Consequently, *La Prensa* was also prohibited from publishing interviews with Robelo and with Rafael Córdova Rivas and Arturo Cruz, two members of the five-man Junta. The interviews concerned the banned political meeting, and both Junta members were critical of the government's action. Of course, all this had nothing to do with "national security."

After the Sandinistas and their sympathizers had left *La Prensa* in May 1980, we made an honest effort to avoid confrontational politics. The editorial staff had many meetings discussing how we could moderate any criticisms, and we explored ways to avoid provoking the government's anger. We were not always successful, but it was in our interest not to antagonize the government. The Sandinistas, however, violently attacked our mildest criticisms. We were soon typecast as "the voice of the bourgeoisie," "counterrevolutionary schemers," and that perennial catchall—"the hidden hand of the CIA." The Sandinista-controlled media invented some bizarre theories to explain how sinister and subversive *La Prensa* had become. They mounted a massive disinformation campaign against *La Prensa*, and they were helped by the large number of foreign sympathizers (the so-called "internationalists") who work and live in Nicaragua.

In a series of articles published in *Barricada* and *El Nuevo Diario*, a North American claimed we were using techniques supposedly used by the *Daily Gleaner* in Jamaica and *El Mercurio* in Chile to undermine the respective governments of Michael Manley and Salvador Allende. These charges were then publicized by Sandinista agents and sympathizers abroad. *La Prensa* was thus supposedly running sensationalist stories to alienate the people from the government. In addition, and this is the heart of the *Daily Gleaner-El Mercurio-La Prensa* "connection," we were supposedly publishing "subliminal" anti-Sandinista messages and photos that supposedly affected the reader on a subconscious level. It was never explained how, with all the pressure to meet deadlines and turn out a daily paper, we could simultaneously employ subtle, subliminal methods to "destabilize" the government. But a smear campaign never proves anything; it relies on character assassination by assertion.

The Sandinista-dominated National Autonomous University of Nicaragua (UNAN), in conjunction with several "internationalists," most of them Chilean, also published a pamphlet, financed by the government, supposedly proving that *La Prensa* was "counterrevolutionary" and had received advice and counsel from *El Mercurio*. From 1980 on, the Sandinistas continued to make these vague and calumnious accusations.

But as *La Prensa* had to submit to *prior* censorship from March 1982 to June 1986, how were we able to publish all these "sensationalist" and "subliminal" messages and hence threaten the Sandinista government? The Sandinistas simply ignored the contradictions in their slanders. Perhaps the "subliminal" messages also affected the Sandinista censors, causing them to ignore the subversive, anti-Sandinista propaganda, hence turning them into unwitting CIA agents tricked into destabilizing the Sandinista regime. We at *La Prensa* never saw a copy of *El Mercurio* let alone the *Daily Gleaner*, but we are willing to entertain any forthcoming leftwing fantasies about how we destabilized the censors and thus threatened "national security."

As 1980 ended, all the independent Nicaraguan media had either been censored, closed, or destroyed, as well as subjected to government disinformation campaigns. In retrospect, this is not surprising. After all, eight days after the Sandinistas took power, Cuban military and security advisers arrived in Nicaragua; one month later, Soviet generals paid a secret visit to Managua and hundreds of Nicaraguan children were being sent to Cuba's Isle of Youth for political indoctrination. Within days after the Sandinistas entered Managua, representatives from international terrorist organizations, such as the *Monteneros* and the PLO, arrived in Nicaragua to set up liaisons with the Sandinistas. In September 1979, the FSLN leadership had met secretly and formulated the infamous "72-hour Document," which sets forth a Leninist program for consolidating power and organizing all forces "under the leadership of the FSLN." In the first year of Sandinista power, they created a partisan Party army, a Party police force, a Party network of block spies (copied from Cuba), and two partisan Party unions that coercively co-opted many independent unions. In addition, the Sandinistas had arbitrarily changed the composition of the Council of State and had contrived the political assassination of Jorge Salazar, leader of COSEP—an umbrella organization of independent businesses. One of the most popular FSLN slogans was and remains "National Directorate, order us" (*Dirección Nacional, Ordene!*)—a cheap clone of Cuba's Stalinist slogan, "Commander-in-chief [Castro] order us!"

The Institutionalization of Repression

THE YEAR 1981 marks the formal institutionalization of the systematic repression of *La Prensa*. By then, the Governing Junta had been reduced from five members to three, all of them Sandinistas, under the coordination of Comandante Daniel Ortega; and the Media Office had been attached to Comandante Tomás Borge's Ministry of Interior. The Sandinista censor was Lt. Michelle Najlis.

With the repression and the shutdowns of *La Prensa*, the Nicaraguan people felt themselves to be limited in their right to be informed and to express themselves. At the same time, democratic countries that had previously supported the Sandinistas began to have misgivings.

Comparisons of the past Somocista dictatorship with the present Sandinista government were also inevitable. By this time, it was already a notorious public fact that the Sandinistas had abandoned all promises of democracy in order to implant a Marxist-Leninist state.

The following are the threats and shutdowns of *La Prensa* by the Sandinista state in 1981 (notice that there were already a series of preordained subjects that could not be published):

5 January 1981: Media Office directive, forbidding "news, printed ads, editorial comments, and letters to the editor, etc." on the country's banana production and the negotiations which were then going on with the Standard Fruit Company. It was also forbidden to publish the prohibition order.

20 January: Media Office directive, forbidding news and comments on rising sugar and rice prices. Again, it was also forbidden to publish the prohibition order.

22 January: Warning from the Media Office, for having published an AP dispatch on the detention of Nicaraguan Air Force officers in the United States. The Media Office alleged that it was forbidden under Decree #511.

10 February: Prohibition of any news or comments on the government's temporary closing of the Permanent Commission on Human Rights (CPDH), the only independent human rights organization in Nicaragua.

10 July: First shutdown of *La Prensa* for forty-eight hours, by order of the Media Office, alleging that news published on 7 July was untrue. We had published photos and an editorial lamenting the destruction of religious billboards by unknown vandals.

25 July: Warning for having published a letter and cartoons alluding to Comandante Zero, Edén Pastora. Since 14 July any mention of Pastora was prohibited.

29 July: Second shutdown of *La Prensa* for forty-eight hours, by order of the Media Office, alleging that on that day, we had shown disrespect for Carlos Fonseca Amador (one of the founders of the FSLN) in an article on British Prince Charles' wedding. (See Appendix A.)

3 August: Prohibition of a department store ad, because the drawing showed a girl in shorts. According to the Media Office, such drawing "makes use of women as sexual objects." The same Media Office lifted the prohibition after a letter from *La Prensa* explained that we were not violating any Media Law, because since the advertisement dealt with women's shorts, this was the only way it could appear.

19 August: Third shutdown of *La Prensa* for seventy-two hours, by order of the Media Office, for having published a foreign dispatch with statements by Foreign Minister Miguel D'Escoto, which the Media Office alleged were absolutely false. *La Prensa* afterwards demonstrated that D'Escoto had made those statements.

28 September: Warning because of an "El Pimpollito" Restaurant ad which, according to the Media Office, promoted the consumption of liquors.

28 September: The Media Office demanded that *La Prensa* present proof that the assertions made by an industrialist in an interview published the day before were true.

28 September: The Media Office ordered the suspension of the Intercontinental Hotel ads, because, according to its interpretation, they promoted the consumption of liquor.

29 September: Fourth shutdown for twenty-four hours, by order of the

Media Office, alleging that the industrialist's interview published on 27 September contained charges against government functionaries which jeopardized the economic stability of the nation.

1 October: Fifth shutdown for forty-eight hours, by order of the Media Office, alleging that our defense of the 27 September interview was a repetition of the same "crime" for which *La Prensa* had been previously suspended. After the fifth shutdown, the government informed us that we were in a state of political confrontation and, if we continued, we would be definitively closed.

Beginning on 9 September and for a period of one year, the "Economic and Social Emergency Law" (Decree #812) established a State of Emergency in Nicaragua, imposing penalties of one to three years in prison for "false" publications tending to alter prices, salaries, foodstuffs, clothes, merchandise, shares, titles, and currency. In essence, this law allowed the executive power to suspend totally the rights and guarantees of the Nicaraguan people throughout the entire country or in parts thereof. It placed natural catastrophes and economic difficulties due to inefficient administration on equal footing. News relating to either was prohibited. At the same time, this decree classified certain deeds as crimes against the Economic and Social Security of the Nation. Some acts, if not all, had been included before in Chapter XII, title IV of the Penal Code, thereby effectively increasing the penalties while decreasing the precarious freedom of the press that then existed. Press freedom was, of course, additionally threatened by Decrees #511 and #512, in effect since September 1980, and which, by themselves, virtually made press freedom a fiction in Nicaragua.

In the same month, we were forbidden to publish an opinion poll of nine hundred people which showed the government losing the support of the people. The Census and Statistics National Institute (INEC) based the prohibition on Decree #102 of 4 October 1979, which is the law that created the National Statistics System and the Census and Statistics National Institute. That decree, however, doesn't authorize the director of the Institute to forbid publication of polls or statistics; consequently, *La Prensa* asked the Supreme Court of Justice to rescind the prohibition. But before the Supreme Court could rule, the government hastily brought a new law before the Council of State, empowering the Institute to forbid both the taking and the publication of polls not authorized by it or the publication of any statistics whatsoever (Decree #888, 7 December 1981). Since INEC controls all statistical information in Nicaragua, it controls statistical "reality"—hence all the glowing government reports and their corresponding cooked figures about health care, literacy, and other assorted myths.

It would be tedious to narrate each shutdown in detail. The repressive measures, the dates, and the documented facts themselves are sufficient; but we must stress that we were not allowed the right of defense or appeal in any of the cases and, therefore, we were defenseless. The orders were drastic and immediate, as in the famous epitaph of the Mexican Revolution: Shoot him dead first and inquire later!

A *locus classicus* of Sandinista censorship occurred during the third shutdown, by order of the Media Office, on 19 August 1981, suspending the publication and circulation of three consecutive issues, those of 20, 21, and 22 August. The motive was the reproduction of an interview of the Sandinista foreign minister, Miguel D'Escoto, published by *El Periódico* newspaper in Mexico City, and reproduced in turn by newspapers in Costa Rica, Panama, and other Hispanic-American countries. *La Prensa* added some of its own interviews of people alluded to by D'Escoto, as well as one with D'Escoto himself, who insisted that he hadn't made those statements. D'Escoto had accused Miguel Obando y Bravo, archbishop of Managua, of being the leading "counterrevolutionary" in Nicaragua. The Media Office reacted by ordering the suspension of *La Prensa* for three days.

La Prensa subsequently proved and demonstrated that D'Escoto had in fact made the statements. The very journalist who had interviewed him asserted that D'Escoto had made those statements to him several months earlier while attending an international conference in India. But they were not published until later, on the occasion of Foreign Minister D'Escoto's visit to Mexico, and as evidence the journalist offered the tape on which the interview had originally been recorded. *El Periódico*, in Mexico, then published the interview, confirmed the existence of the statements, and expressed surprise that D'Escoto now denied them.

The shutdowns of *La Prensa* produced financial losses and forced us to exercise a form of self-censorship. One of our newspaper's staff members had the special duty of reading the entire copy and pointing out any "dangerous" news or commentary. But despite this auto-censorship and the closings, *La Prensa* remained a vigorous and informative newspaper. Indeed, after each shutdown, twice as many papers were printed and circulated the next day because of the heightened interest and favorable reception of the Nicaraguan people. This irritated the Sandinistas, for both of their subsidized newspapers, *Barricada* and *El Nuevo Diario*, sold many fewer newspapers. *(La Prensa* was the only newspaper that had its circulation certified.)

There is no doubt, as Daniel Ortega had put it, that the Sandinistas wished we would "disappear." We published government pronouncements and asked questions about deviations from the original pledges and guarantees made by the Sandinistas; we questioned the Sandinistas' identification of the state with their Party, as well as their support of Soviet foreign policy. In a popular cartoon strip, we made reference to the comandantes' penchant for Mercedes Benzes and luxurious mansions. Meanwhile, the Sandinistas kept up a variety of incessant smear campaigns against *La Prensa*, and we soon noted an emerging pattern. First, instead of debating or refuting our ideas and criticisms, the Sandinistas responded with *ad hominem* slanders, accusing us of being "counterrevolutionaries," "traitors," "CIA agents," and a host of other predictable epithets, characteristic of Marxist-Leninist tirades. Second, even when we focused on sports or events in no way political or objectionable to the regime, the Sandinistas accused us of "ideological diversionism"—a phrase borrowed again from Cuba, suggesting bourgeois escapism, distracting "the people" from their "revolutionary" priorities. It was all so neat. Anything in *La Prensa* could be labeled "counterrevolutionary." The only option they left us was to parrot the government's line and become a puppet newspaper. But as we saw that both *Barricada* and *El Nuevo Diario* were subsidized by the government and that the former was staffed by foreign "internationalists," we took satisfaction in the fact that we were publishing an independent newspaper by and for the Nicaraguan people.

The government then tried to boycott *La Prensa* economically. Since the vast majority of all advertisements were published in *La Prensa*, the government prohibited all state agencies from advertising in our newspaper. In addition, anyone connected or associated with the Sandinistas was told by them not to submit any artistic endeavors to *La Prensa Literaria*, the *La Prensa* literary supplement that appeared on weekends. Almost all the Sandinistas with literary interests had previously published in *La Prensa Literaria*, including Ernesto Cardenal, Sergio Ramírez, Rosario Murillo, and Carlos Mejía Godoy.

In December 1981, we published a revealing memo that was leaked to us. The memo was signed by Federico López, head of the FSLN department of Mass Media, and addressed to the managers and editors of the state-controlled media. The memo, whose authorship the FSLN could not deny, gave instructions on how to deal with news about Poland and that government's problems with the independent union, *Solidarity*. We reproduce it in full:

"YEAR OF THE DEFENSE AND THE PRODUCTION"
Managua, December 17, 1981

Dear Comrades:
Due to the delicate social situation that our sister country of Poland is going through and the manipulation of information by the imperialist news agencies, we suggest that our coverage of the problem be oriented along the following lines:

1. Do not give space to the versions transmitted by the news agencies controlled by imperialism, because they tend to create false expectations; they manipulate concrete facts to disseminate their anti-Soviet and anti-Communist views; moreover, they spread "reliable" versions given by persons "close to official sources," etc., by which means they confuse the public and brazenly lie.

2. Reflect the difficult situation that faces the Polish revolutionary movement from an objective viewpoint, reporting only those facts that have been confirmed by the TASS and [Castro's Cuban] *Prensa Latina* news agencies. It is not a question of concealing information, but of being responsible with that information.

3. Stress that the emergency measures taken by the Party and the Government in Poland are aimed at rescuing the country from the crisis created in Poland by the violation of socialist principles on the part of some ex-leaders of the union (today under arrest) and the manipulation of these errors by the counterrevolution directed by imperialism, but as reported by the Polish and Socialist leaders and press. They are not repressing the workers but only the counterrevolutionary elements that wish to hand over Poland to imperialism. The question is to insure social peace in order to overcome the crisis. It shouldn't be stressed that strikes are forbidden, but that a call is being made to confront the economic crisis.

4. Stress the positive elements that the situation reflects: the peace, stability, and order imposed. The reactionaries are inventing "shootings," "exchange of shots," etc.

5. Neutralize the tendency to present the Polish government as "the new military government," or the "Soviet presence," stressing that it is up to the Polish people to solve the matter. Stress statements along that line by some Western leaders.

6. Utilize the Polish government's willingness to have a dialogue. This is fundamental.

7. Although it is not possible to neutralize the reactionaries' anti-Sovietism in reference to Poland, we can neutralize the possible analogies that the reactionaries may make between Nicaragua and Poland, especially with regard to the strikes.

It is necessary to develop a line that stresses the freedom that exists in our country, the democracy, the accomplishments, etc.

Certain of your attention to this letter, a fraternal greeting.

FREE COUNTRY OR DEATH
(Signed) Federico López
Media Section
D.E.P.E.P. [Department of Propaganda and Political Education of the Sandinista Party].

In effect, the government was directing its controlled media how to report and respond according to a preconceived governmental line. Even more ominous was the first appearance of the mobs the Sandinistas use to intimidate and terrorize people. The Sandinistas call them *turbas divinas* ("divine mobs"), and they are controlled and directed by the government, which has copied Somoza's *Nicolasa*.

For the sheer power to intimidate, however, the Sandinista *turbas* far surpass their predecessors. On repeated occasions they attacked *La Prensa* installations and besieged the homes of its owners and functionaries (including my own, and those of the widow, son, and mother of Pedro Joaquín Chamorro Cardenal), throwing stones, painting obscene words and slogans on the walls, pounding on doors, and screaming insults at the people inside. Only after they grew tired, or when the "operation" was considered finished, would the attackers finally depart, leaving behind defaced walls, broken windows, smashed vehicles, and terrorized victims. Since the mobs were protected by the police and led by one or another Sandinista functionary —sometimes a man, at other times a woman—they could attack with impunity.

One of the first mob attacks occurred on 13 February 1981, when the Sandinistas unleashed the *turbas* on a group of opposition leaders and a large crowd that had turned out to meet José Esteban González, head of the only independent human rights organization in Nicaragua, at the Augusto César Sandino airport in Managua. Among the many people beaten were Fabio Gadea, owner of three independent radio stations, and Oscar Montalván, a well-known journalist for *Radio Mil*. The car of a *La Prensa* chauffeur, Mauricio Orozco, was also destroyed by the mobs. On 10 March, the *turbas* struck again, destroying the MDN headquarters in Managua. In addition, the *turbas* began threatening many of our distributors in the remote towns and provinces throughout the country, forcing some of them to give up selling *La Prensa*.

On 16 March, the night Sandinista mobs broke up a legal meeting held by the Nicaraguan Democratic Movement (MDN), there was a series of coordinated mob actions against *La Prensa* employees in various parts of the country. In Managua, a mob stood in front of the house of Humberto Belli, our editorial page editor, and shouted Sandinista slogans and threats; another mob slashed the tires of a car owned by Roberto Cardenal, assistant to the editor and secretary of the editorial staff.

In addition, Abelardo Sánchez, a *La Prensa* correspondent in Ocotal, was the victim of a massive campaign in the Sandinista press. Sánchez was arrested by the FSLN and condemned on 16 June as a "counterrevolutionary." He was sentenced to three years in prison. During this time he was brutally abused, and when he was finally released he was in deplorable condition.

Máximo Alonso, our León correspondent, was attacked and beaten by a Sandinista mob on the premises of the León Court House on 30 June 1981. This was followed by the threat of further mob violence against him and his family at home. Víctor Medina, a Managua reporter, was harassed in October 1981 by Sandinista State Security agents on the premises of the Sandinista Council of State. This Sandinista operation was ordered by Federico López who was also an FSLN representative in the Council of State. Auxiliadora Echegoyen, another Managua reporter, was threatened by a Sandinista mob in the dead of night with loudspeakers blaring promises of a firing squad. She was apprehended without charge and interrogated during the early morning hours at "House No. 50," a notorious FSLN interrogation center.

On 30 December, the Ministry of Interior prohibited any reports or information about the Atlantic Coast that had not been issued by the government itself, thus doubly sealing off the Miskito, Sumo, and Rama Indians from the outside world. Now access to the Atlantic Coast was possible only through government aegis. Our reporters, of course, were prohibited from traveling to the Atlantic Coast.

As 1981 ended, it was clear that the revolution thousands of Nicaraguans had paid for with their own blood had been betrayed. In August 1981, Humberto Ortega, minister of defense, addressed an elite army unit and declared that the Sandinista revolution is "profoundly anti-imperialist, anti-Yankee, and Marxist-Leninist." By this time, the Sandinistas had set up a vast network of prisons, and the Nicaraguan people were experiencing daily the most intense levels of oppression in our country's history. But even that oppression would increase in 1982.

Assault on *La Prensa*

IN JANUARY 1982, *La Prensa* was closed and occupied militarily for three days. But in order to do this, the Sandinistas orchestrated a series of events leading to the takeover. On 9 January the Ministry of Interior announced that a counterrevolutionary plot to dynamite a petroleum refinery and assassinate various Sandinista leaders had been discovered. Tomás Borge implicated a group of people, some of them Nicaraguans, including José Esteban González, the former head of CPDH who had been forced into exile, and Adriana Guillén, a reporter for *La Prensa*.

Guillén was our correspondent in Costa Rica. She had formerly been a Sandinista but had broken with them in 1980, when she saw the revolution being betrayed. Bayardo Arce took this personally and told her sister that Adriana should leave *La Prensa* or she might end up like Jorge Salazar—the leader of COSEP who was set up and murdered by the Sandinistas in 1980. For this reason, we had her transferred to Costa Rica. In Costa Rica, Adriana and José Esteban González had become concerned with the Sandinistas' oppression of the Miskito Indians and were documenting Sandinista atrocities.

Meanwhile, back in Managua, all those in opposition to the Sandinistas were preparing for a march on 10 January in honor of Pedro Joaquín Chamorro, who had been murdered on the same date three years earlier. But the Sandinistas intended to distract attention from the march. In the 10 January issue of *La Prensa*, we ran a news item from the Spanish news agency EFE. In it, EFE quoted a news item that appeared in the Soviet news agency TASS. The TASS source was, not surprisingly, the

La Prensa

TASS correspondent in Managua. According to this correspondent, "various directors of the ultraright newspaper *La Prensa* were among the antigovernment conspirators recently discovered by Nicaraguan state security."

There was a pattern developing. The day before the march in honor of Pedro Joaquín the Sandinistas announced a conspiracy and named, among others, a *La Prensa* correspondent. Their stratagem was, of course, to indirectly implicate *La Prensa* in the "conspiracy" and simultaneously discredit both Adriana Guillén and José Esteban González and their documentation of Sandinista atrocities. Accused by the government of conspiring to dynamite plants and murder Sandinista leaders and additionally, for good measure, of having links with Negro Chamorro, the anti-Sandinista fighter, Adriana could not return to Nicaragua. She was forced into exile.

Next, an item appeared in TASS accusing unnamed directors of *La Prensa* of participating in the conspiracy. The announcement of the "plot" occurred one day before a massive march by the opposition. Thus it was clear to us that the Sandinistas were attempting to deflect attention from the march and settle some old political scores by implicating *La Prensa* and various members of the Venezuelan embassy—an embassy that had been supportive of *La Prensa* and that had planned to open a cultural center that would facilitate freedom of speech.

On 10 January, the day of the march in support of Pedro Joaquín, a Sandinista mob, armed with rocks and sticks, attacked a group of people who had gathered at Pedro Joaquín's grave to honor his memory. But the Sandinistas were not through. On 13 January, at the height of the "conspiracy" campaign, the Sandinistas organized a demonstration against *La Prensa*. They marched a Sandinista mob in front of *La Prensa* at about 5:30 P.M., after we had closed. The only people inside were three of our security guards armed respectively with a rifle, a .38, and a Magnum .357. The mob shouted insults and Sandinista slogans at the guards and pelted them with rocks and fruit. They then tried to forcibly enter *La Prensa*, causing two of the guards to fire their pistols in the air and then turn a fire hose on the crowd. This enraged the mob leaders who ordered an assault. The guard with the Magnum .357 fired and missed one of the leaders, but the other guards did not fire at all. In the general confusion, shots were fired by unidentified persons and two people were injured. Suddenly, Sandinista Security forces arrived on the scene and occupied *La Prensa*, arresting the three guards.

Following this incident, Tomás Borge summoned me and two other editors, Pablo Antonio Cuadra and Pedro Joaquín Chamorro Barrios, to his office and made the following proposal: if *La Prensa* agreed to condemn the security guards for assaulting people who were peacefully protesting *La Prensa*'s "counterrevolutionary attitude," the newspaper (still occupied by Sandinista police) would be returned to us and the security guards would not be punished. We told Borge that while we regretted what had happened, the security guards were only doing their job and their weapons had been duly registered with the Sandinista police. Subsequently, there was a trial, and *La Prensa* took over the guards' defense.

On 14 January, the government declared that any public commentary or information about "the incidents that took place at *La Prensa*" had to be "confirmed" by the government. In effect, the government controlled the public flow of pertinent information. On the same day, the *La Prensa* security guard with the .38 confessed to firing it. But later in court, he revealed he had been forced into making this confession. We also established that one person had been wounded by a .38 and the other by a .22. Only the security guard with the Magnum had fired his weapon at the mob. Moreover, a state ballistic expert testified that the incriminating bullets had not been fired from our security guards' pistols. The government's contention that our security guards had wounded them was absurd. We obviously suspected that someone fired the pistols to implicate *La Prensa*. But despite these and other discrepancies in the government's case, two of the guards were sentenced to three-year terms, half of which they served in prison and the other half on parole.

In the meantime, the military occupation of *La Prensa* had lasted for three days. Since the security guards were in jail, there was no legal justification for the takeover, but the Sandinistas had their own motives. They used the time to go through *La Prensa*'s archives and make extensive photocopies of what they found there. (At least 2,000 copies were made, according to the meter we had on *La Prensa*'s Xerox machine.) They also brought in expert locksmiths who forced open locked doors and desk drawers, as we found out when we finally got back to our offices and discovered that most of the documents in our files had been rearranged. In the end, it seemed appropriate that on 13 January, the day *La Prensa* was assaulted, Tomás Borge declared that "miracles were forbidden." Any news or information relating to miracles or supernatural events were "totally prohibited" until the church had proved them or until, as we surmised from the case of *La Prensa* guards convicted of miraculously wounding two people with weapons they did not fire, Tomás Borge personally corroborated them.

La Prensa

On another occasion, three of us working late at the paper were forced to spend the night in our offices because the mob, attacking after the work day was over, prevented us from leaving. During this particular siege, the chief of a Sandinista patrol arrived on the scene and told me not to worry, nothing would happen because he was on the job (supposedly to protect *La Prensa* from the mob, but in reality to supervise them). All in all some 20 percent of *La Prensa*'s employees left the country during this period due to threats or acts of physical violence against them.

The Sandinistas also used the mobs to attack the distribution points throughout Nicaragua where *La Prensa* was sold. Forty of the agencies had been forced to stop selling *La Prensa* by 26 June 1986, because their owners and employees had been harassed, threatened, or beaten. Thus it was not only freedom of the press that was (and is) threatened in Nicaragua, but also the freedom to work, since many people made their living selling the paper.

AGENTS OF *LA PRENSA* WHO HAVE SUFFERED REPRESSION
(From Homes Defaced with Graffiti to Arrests and Jail)

The following synoptic table is representative of the aggressions and repressions suffered by *La Prensa*'s agencies and agents throughout Nicaragua. Out of 157 departmental agencies outside Managua, 40 were forced to shut down, leaving 117 active: of these 117, 45 had been seriously threatened, and almost all were forced to remove *La Prensa* identification signs or posters. The synoptic table was taken from *La Prensa* files shortly before the Sandinistas closed *La Prensa* on 26 June 1986.

AGENCY LOCATION	ISSUES SOLD	AGENT'S NAME	TYPE OF REPRESSION
Cuidad Rama	100	Santos Martínez	Imprisoned, demonstrations in front of his home, graffiti on it and on *La Prensa*'s sign. Constant threats.
Cuapa	15	Enrique Winter	Graffiti on his home and threats from the mobs.

Assault on La Prensa

Agency Location	Issues Sold	Agent's Name	Type of Repression
El Coral	25	Carmen de Centeno	Her home was assaulted and looted by mobs bearing army weapons; has been constantly harassed.
Nueva Guinea	90	Jaime Rodríguez	He is in hiding because he is being persecuted; his wife now runs the agency.
Esquipulas-Matagalpa	40	Jesús Martínez	He was under arrest, has a business, and suffered an assault—he is constantly harassed.
Río Blanco	150	Alonso Bracamonte	He was taken prisoner, freed under the condition that he would present himself daily at headquarters. He is being forced to inform against his son who left town. They are forcing him to go to Honduras to locate his son.
Mina El Limón	30	Alejandro Baldelomar	Harassment and threats.
Chichigalpa	500	Mariana de Baltodano	Graffiti on her home and threats from Sandinista mass organizations.
El Viejo	300	Gonzalo Ulloa	Graffiti on his

La Prensa

Agency Location	Issues Sold	Agent's Name	Type of Repression
			home, has been threatened with death.
Corinto	550	Mayra Patricia de Gómez	Demonstrations in front of her home, threats of burning it. Agent's father constantly in jail, where he is pressured to stop selling *La Prensa*.
Somotillo	40	Pedro Reyes	Threats and harassment.
Altagracia	60	Yelba Potoy de Gómez	Threats and harassment.
Masatepe	190	Silvia de Lacayo	Graffiti on her home.
Masaya	2100	Vilma Robles	Graffiti on her home.
Muhan	25	Elvis Dávila	Jailed twice.
Los Santos	12	Elisa Lazo de Flores	She decided to shut down, afraid of her own son, a Sandinista soldier, who threatened to burn her home if she continued selling the paper. The son already gave a house of hers in Muhan to internationalists.
Telpaneca	50	Guillermo Ardón	They confiscated his property. He is

Assault on La Prensa

Agency Location	Issues Sold	Agent's Name	Type of Repression
			a very old man on the brink of desperation, living under constant threats.
San Juan del Río Coco	100	Tolentino Rodríguez	Harassment and threats.
San Ramón Matagalpa	35	Edmundo Palacios	They put him in jail and continue threatening him.
Ticuantepe	70	Pablo Morales	Harassment and threats.
Apascali, Golfo de Fonseca	30	Jorge Baldelomar	They put him in jail and threaten him constantly.
Moyogalpa	40	Orlando Romero	Harassment.
El Crucero	120	María Luisa Rodríguez	The mobs assaulted the agent and also the truck transporting *La Prensa*.
Rosita, Zelaya	80	Julio Osejo	Harassment and threats.
El Salto	25	Julio Molina	Threatened.
San Lucas, Somoto	15	Edgard Pinell	Threatened by the mobs.
El Jicaral	10	Sergio Juárez	Threatened by the mobs.
La Concordia	10	José Francisco Zeledón	Threatened by the mobs.

La Prensa

Agency Location	Issues Sold	Agent's Name	Type of Repression
Santo Tomás del Norte	10	Clementina Tabora	One of her sons was put in jail, and she received constant threats.
Santa Lucía	12	Marcial Escobar	Threats by the mobs.
Santa Clara, Nueva Segovia	15	Miguel Aguilar	Threats by the mobs.
Ingenio Julio Buitrago (Montelimar)	30	Gilberto Barberena	Threats by the mobs.
Ingenio Monterrosa	60	Carlos Zamora	Fired from his job for selling *La Prensa*.
Susucayán	25	Elba López	War zone; threatened by the mobs.
El Realejo	20	Reynaldo Bustamante	Threats from the mass organizations.
Teotecacinte	25	Estanislao Fuentes	Threats from the mass organizations.
San Fernando	15	Lucila de Beteta	Threats from the mass organizations.
Potosí, Golfo de Fonseca	20	Adolfo Matute Flores	Threats from the mass organizations.
Mozonte	20	Oscar Bustamante	Threats from the mass organizations.
Matiguás	150	Esmeralda Treminio	She was under arrest and received serious threats.

We were also told by a number of *La Prensa* agents that some of the people who turned up in these mobs had made a living doing the same thing under Somoza. This willingness to welcome back old Somocistas seems to be a fundamental characteristic of *Sandinismo*. Many of the same thugs who once worked for Somoza now fill the state agencies and are successfully integrated into the Sandinista Defense Committees and other government positions where their services are appreciated. That is why many of us in Nicaragua say that *Sandinismo* is *Somocismo* of the Left; it is scientific *Somocismo*.

In Bluefields, on the Atlantic Coast, on 13 January—the very day the mobs attacked *La Prensa*—the State Security police confiscated all copies of that day's *La Prensa* before they could be distributed. We, of course, vigorously protested this illegal confiscation, but to no avail. On 19 January, the military officer in charge of the town of Rama refused to let our distributors proceed up the river to Bluefields. From that point on, our employees on the Atlantic Coast were periodically prevented from delivering *La Prensa*. In addition to being constantly harassed and imprisoned on various occasions, they were offered money (which they did not accept) to stop selling *La Prensa*. Our reporters had, of course, been forbidden to visit the Atlantic Coast since October 1980.

On 18 January, Sandinista mobs defaced Violeta Chamorro's house, besmirching it with crude slogans and caricatures.

On 26 January, Comandante Tomás Borge held a two-hour press conference in which he accused *La Prensa* of having links with the CIA. As usual, the allegations were vague and unsubstantiated. Borge had to publicly admit, however, that *La Prensa* had by far the highest circulation of the three newspapers, but he attributed this to the people's curiosity—something comparable to a harmful vice that affected a person's health.

At the same time, Comandante Jaime Wheelock asserted that *La Prensa* played the principal role in disseminating "counterrevolutionary ideas to fool and confuse the people." We replied by publicly asking the comandante to provide specifics. Like all the Sandinistas, Wheelock was more comfortable with slander than accuracy; he did not respond.

The month of January 1982 demonstrated that the Sandinistas (having closed two radio stations and suspended nine news programs) had decided to launch a systematic assault on the independent media—an assault that would culminate two months later in the declaration of a state of emergency and prior censorship.

During the first two to three years that the Sandinistas controlled Nicaragua, an external opposition had begun to take shape. At the beginning, it consisted mainly of former members of Somoza's despised National Guard, assisted by the government of Argentina. The Argentines were soon replaced by the CIA, which began pumping money into the opposition army or Contras, as the Sandinistas called them. Contra ranks then began swelling with poor *campesinos* who were angry and disaffected with Sandinista rule. In contrast with the essentially middle-class composition of Sandinista military units during the war against Somoza, the Contras are essentially a peasant army.

On 14 March 1982, the Contras blew up two bridges near the Honduran border. On 15 March 1982 the government declared a state of emergency, suspending a series of rights and guarantees, some of which had already been suspended in practice. Radio newscasts and political party opinion programs were prohibited and all radio stations had to link up every six hours with a government radio network. In addition, Lt. Nelba Cecilia Blandón, the new Sandinista censor, felt obliged to issue her own decree, requiring all media, both written and broadcast, to submit their daily programs or editorial copy for prior censorship. As on the Atlantic coast, we were prohibited from ever sending our reporters into the war zone, while *El Nuevo Diario* and *Barricada* had free access. Thus, we were deprived of reporting a major event that had major implications for our country.

On 16 March, we received the following communiqués from the Censorship Bureau:

March 16, 1982
"Year of the Unity Against Aggression"
Mr. Carlos Holmann
Board of Directors, *La Prensa* Newspaper

Sir:
The Media Office informs you that you must not leave blank spaces in your newspaper, and you must also not mention that what you publish has been approved by us.

We thank you in a special manner for the assistance that you have given to this office so that we may carry out our work well.
Sincerely,
(Signed) Nelba Blandón
Director of Communications Media
Republic of Nicaragua-Interior Ministry-Media Office
(Seal)

March 16, 1982
COMMUNICATIONS MEDIA OFFICE ORDERS THE FOLLOWING:
Page 9 Change the title: "U.S. presents plan to control Contras" to the following: "Haig Presents U.S. Proposal."
In the introduction, eliminate the riders that say: "EDITED UNDER CENSORSHIP," likewise the other rider that says: "EDITED UNDER EMERGENCY LAW."
COMMUNICATIONS MEDIA OFFICE

On 24 March we were unable to publish due to excessive prior censorship, ironically justified by the Ministry of Interior which announced, "the policy of truth is the policy of the Revolution." On 28 March, all news about the elections in El Salvador was censored. Since the dispatches were from international news agencies like UPI, the Sandinistas insisted they were not true. Because of the excessive censorship, we decided not to publish that day's edition. On 9 August, we were forbidden to publish a Papal communiqué. On 11 and 12 August we could not publish for the same reason. On 18 November, we could not publish because of excessive censorship, and on 24 and 25 November, *La Prensa* was shut down by the government for printing censored material. There had been a typesetting error and, consequently, a *Miami Herald* article was published, signed by Jack Anderson, under the title "Palestinian Capers," telling of the existence of girls of "doubtful reputation" in the USSR and the love affairs they have had with PLO fighters training in the Soviet Union. It had been censored. We acknowledged that we had committed an inadvertent error when we let it go by, but we had not done it intentionally. Had we wished to evade censorship, we wouldn't have chosen such an irrelevant article to do so; we would have chosen a much more important article or news item, at least one related to current events in Nicaragua.

Nevertheless, the sanction went beyond this small error, and thus the censor made the following accusation: "*La Prensa* has been showing an antipatriotic and provocative attitude, as the following facts illustrate: Its decision not to publish on several occasions in order to lend arguments to the enemies of our people that may justify any aggression against our revolution." The censor then declared that, from that date on (and without any legal justification), it would be a crime to distribute censored items and the "...surreptitious spreading of items the publication of which has not been authorized by this Office." The censor didn't specify that the material in question was an item about the Soviet Union, but her words made sense only in reference to Jack Anderson's article on the PLO.

The censor also suppressed an explanation to our readers on why there had been no *La Prensa* the day before. In that explanation, besides stating why we had failed to publish the paper on several previous occasions due to excessive censorship and the late hour in which we received the censor's communiqué, we had responded: "Your second argument for suspending publication is 'the surreptitious spreading of items the publication of which has not been authorized by this Office.' Although the accusation is vague and imprecise, we suppose that you are referring to the fact that *La Prensa* sends censored items to some embassies (the Soviet, among others), to political parties, and democratic organizations, etc."

"If that is the case, if that is the accusation you make, we wish to tell you that censorship of a newspaper is one thing, and censorship of private correspondence is something else. Decree #996, to which you make reference, doesn't authorize you to censor our correspondence; therefore, we are making use of our rights as citizens when we send written communications by mail or messenger. The envelopes in which we send *La Prensa*'s correspondence are duly identified with the newspaper's letterhead, and have, besides, the full address of the persons to whom they are sent."

Censorship of *La Prensa* was methodically repressive. After we completed the day's edition, three copies of each page (including the advertisements and comic strips) had to be sent to Lieutenant Blandón's office. To this was added two pages of "filler"—materials that, if approved, could be substituted for any materials Blandón censored. In 1982, Blandón usually decided within two hours what could or could not be published, but by 1986, she averaged between four and six hours. In March 1986, it reached the absurd level of six hours and fifty minutes. These long, intentional delays financially hurt *La Prensa*, and work hours had to be increased by 60 percent.

After the censor had "revised" the copy, a letter was sent informing us what could or could not be published. In 1982, we could call in the changes the censor wanted. But afterwards, the Sandinistas had invented a form of double censorship whereby the staff had to make the ordered changes and then send them back to the censor again for her approval. This double censorship added another hour to the prolonged delay. The Sandinistas used censorship to make *La Prensa* both bland and untimely. The two Sandinista newspapers, *Barricada* and *El Nuevo Diario*, were subsidized by the government and appeared early in the morning. With luck, *La Prensa* usually appeared at around seven or eight in the evening, by which time the "news" was either old or diluted. Many times it did not appear until the next morning. It was ironic that directives from the censor carried the heading "Free Nicaragua" and that the Sandinistas used the word "revise" for "censor."

From the time the Sandinistas came to power until 26 June 1986, *La Prensa* was prevented from publishing forty-one times due to excessive censorship. (On several of these occasions, we didn't publish as a protest against their systematic censorship.) Many times, the censorship was so repressive that even the additional filler did not suffice to make up an issue. Moreover, it was forbidden to leave blank spaces where something had been censored or to publish the censor's directives to censor passages. In effect, the censor censored herself. In fact, it was prohibited to allude or to insinuate in any way that *La Prensa* was being censored.

Here are examples of the three types of directives the censor sent: 1. Article (with the theme or news). Resolution: Not to be published. 2. Article: _____. Resolution: Delete paragraphs 3, 4, 5, 6, 16, 17, 18. 3. Article: _____. Resolution: Change the title.

The first of these directives was obviously the most drastic, but the second was not much better, since deleting paragraphs often changed or distorted an article's meaning. Our editors were often forced to withdraw the entire article. At other times, the censor ordered the title to be changed so it would not reflect an article's content. As many readers decide what articles to read by the titles, an inappropriate or misleading title can cause them to skip the article. A typical example of how the Sandinistas distort titles occurred when we published an official proclamation from the Ministry of Industry announcing that industrial production would decrease by 20 percent the following year. We headlined it quite straightforwardly: "Industrial Production Will Decrease 20% Next Year." This was censored. The Sandinistas were finally content with "Future Industrial Production Announced." Of course, this is ideologically petty, but it happens every day in Sandinista Nicaragua.

It happens every day in a country where Edén Pastora must be referred to as "the traitor," where former world-boxing champion Alexis Argüello cannot be mentioned, and where, until recently, the photo of Cardinal Miguel Obando y Bravo was prohibited in newspapers. In fact, the Sandinistas' obsession with Cardinal Obando reached such a level of absurdity that the censor once deleted the word "Cardinals" from a headline we ran about the 1985 World Series, and replaced it with the words "St. Louis."

It is important to note that the Sandinistas literally censored thousands of articles, news items, and titles. Thus we can only offer representative examples of Sandinista censorship that are in no way exhaustive or definitive. Even on the days in which we were able to publish, *La Prensa* was still censored and depended on pages of "filler" and other bland substitutes to make up an issue.

But we had other problems in addition to censorship in 1982. On the evening of 16 April, Violeta B. de Chamorro, widow of Pedro Joaquín, said good night to visitors and then noticed a motorcycle parked right in front of the door of her house. She thought it probably belonged to a young couple relaxing in the Las Palmas park across the street. When her friends left, she went into the kitchen to get some dog food for two police dogs in the back yard where her car was parked. On entering the yard, she turned on the outdoor light. "Imagine my surprise," Doña Violeta says, "when I saw a man inside the Saab (the very car in which my husband Pedro was killed), with the side lights on! 'Who are you?' I screamed, 'What are you doing here?' I kept screaming and I thought, this man is going to kill me like they killed Pedro, and nobody will know who sent him to kill me!"

The man put his hand out and, leaving the car, he walked towards her, saying: "Calm down, woman, let's talk," but she backed toward the house, shouting: "They're going to kill me! Murderer! Thief!" The man turned around, climbed on the car trunk, which was next to the gate, and jumped over the wall out into the street.

Night watchmen at the Ministry of Housing offices a half a block from Doña Violeta's home were making rounds in the neighborhood and saw the man jumping over the wall into the street and gave chase, firing shots into the air. This alerted other people who caught him three blocks away. Doña Violeta was alone at home, but she immediately called her relatives and they, in turn, called the police. The house rapidly filled with policemen. Among some flower pots in the yard, a police helmet was found. Doña Violeta says that she heard a policeman say that the motorcycle belonged to the police. The police immediately carried away the motorcycle and the helmet, but they made a big production out of the investigation. She responded with all the pertinent details to their questioning. They determined that the two police dogs had been drugged.

But nobody ever learned anything about the captured intruder—who he was, what he had declared, or what his motives were.

Long afterwards, in San José, Costa Rica, Doña Violeta met with Claudio Picasso, head of the Investigation Department at Police Headquarters, who had been in charge of the case. He had later defected and fled to Costa Rica. Claudio Picasso told Doña Violeta that at the time he couldn't do anything and that, although her son Carlos Fernando came daily to his office to inquire about the investigation of the case, at the request of his mother, he never dared tell him that Comandante Lenín Cerna, Chief of Sandinista Security, had ordered him not to pursue the case because it would be personally handled by himself and Comandantes Tomás Borge and Walter Ferrety.

Naturally, the "visits at night" at that time were not only in person but also by phone. All the members of *La Prensa*'s board of directors and staff received insulting and threatening phone calls in the early dawn, forcing us to disconnect our phones at night.

On 15 June, Sandinista State Security murdered three students in the neighborhood of San Judas: José Antonio Robleto Palma, 17 years old; Sergio Mercado Madrigal, 20; and Edgar Martín Morales, 18. The Sandinista version was that a "heroic" member of State Security was attacked by the three "antisocials" when he caught them trying to rob a business. But *La Prensa* discovered that the students had been murdered for refusing to join the *turbas* organized by the militant Sandinista youth organization—*Juventud Sandinista 19 de Julio*. We were prohibited from publishing these facts. That night, the infuriated people of the neighborhood marched to the Sandinista bunker (the same bunker that Somoza had occupied) and demanded the bodies. Lenín Cerna, chief of Sandinista Security, gave them the bodies, but he insisted that they be buried the next morning. The people of San Judas, however, buried them the next afternoon, and then 3,000 of them marched through the streets shouting anti-Sandinista slogans.

On 24 June 1982, Horacio Ruiz, one of *La Prensa*'s most respected editors, was forced into his car on a Managua street by four men, two of whom carried machine guns. Ruiz was beaten so severely that he lost consciousness. When he regained consciousness, he was told by one of his assailants, "Now you will find out what the *turbas* are." They then beat him once more, and one of the men with a machine gun threatened to kill him. Finally, Ruiz was driven to a remote spot and thrown out of the car.

La Prensa's account of the attack was partially censored. We were not allowed to mention the machine guns, for instance, or to respond to blatant and absurd discrepancies in the government's version of the incident. (The two government papers, *Barricada* and *El Nuevo Diario*, attempted to write off the attack as the anger of a "jealous husband.") We were also prohibited from mentioning denunciations of the attack that had been carried by various international news agencies.

On 30 June, Pablo Antonio Cuadra, editor-in-chief of *La Prensa*, protested the government's censorship of the assault on Ruiz and sent the following letter to the Government Junta:

Managua, June 30, 1982
Messrs.
Members of the Governing Junta of National Reconstruction
Comandante of the Revolution Daniel Ortega Saavedra
Doctor Sergio Ramírez Mercado
Doctor Rafael Córdova Rivas

Dear Sirs:
After the deplorable assault, kidnapping, and injuries to our editor Horacio Ruiz, *Barricada* and *El Nuevo Diario* published slanderous and offensive versions of the event. The Media Office, however, censored from *La Prensa* all items that would elucidate or help explain the facts, or defend the victim. Indeed, the following articles were suppressed:

On 26 June, two news items: "Police Want to Elucidate Ruiz Case" and "APN [Nicaraguan Journalists' Association] Condemns Attack on Ruiz."

On 27 June, the following articles: "AFP [France Presse News Agency] Supports Ruiz," "Horacio Ruiz Pardons His Detractors," "Questions To Shed Light on Crime Against Horacio Ruiz," and "Horacio Ruiz, Jr. Defends His Father, Horacio Ruiz, Sr., from Infamous Accusations."

In the name of our Editorial Staff, the Board of Directors, and all the workers at *La Prensa*, I protest this unjustifiable denial of the right of defense which is inherent in the very concept of justice, for which reason it can never be abolished in any emergency.

On the other hand, and aggravating the case that motivates our protest, *Barricada*, the official Sandinista newspaper, although aware of the censorship to which we are subjected, made a mockery of journalistic ethics in its *"Al Margen de la Cuartilla"* ["At the Copy Margin"] section, accusing *La Prensa* of abandoning Horacio Ruiz in his misfortune and of remaining silent after manipulating him. If the Media Office censors *Barricada*, as the Media office director affirms, Lt. Blandón—who is the best witness of the news items and articles that she herself has deleted from our paper—should have suppressed the *Barricada* piece because of the profound immorality implicit in the publication of an accusation based on slanders. If *Barricada* is not subject to censorship, the Media Office director still has the obligation of disproving that slander. I consider that the Emergency Law should not be debased to become an instrument of aggressions like this, against the dignity and the rights of man. For that reason, I plead with you to order that these deplorable outrages—that cause so much harm to the image of the Revolution—not be repeated.

                         Sincerely,
                         (signed) Pablo Antonio Cuadra
                         Editor-in-Chief of *La Prensa*.

P.S.—I consider that the easiest and fairest way of disproving the slander that has been published against *La Prensa* is for you to order the Media Office to allow the publication of this letter in our newspaper.

cc: Comandante Tomás Borge M., Minister of the Interior.
Compañera Nelba C. Blandón, Media Office Director.
Files
PAC/can.
(La Prensa Seal)

In the Dominican Republic Sergio Ramírez, a member of the Government Junta, declared on 17 August "that we do not aspire one day to have a free press—we already have a free press in Nicaragua." How often we would hear this, not only from the Sandinistas in their speeches and interviews to foreign audiences and the foreign press—but from the scores of internationalists who were repeating this in their respective countries. Thus, while the Sandinistas had instituted the most systematic press censorship in our country's history and while the Nicaraguan people were suffering the most intense levels of oppression in our nation's history, voices abroad were telling us that we never had it so good—that there was liberty and freedom in Nicaragua, that there was superb education and health care, that the Nicaraguan people enthusiastically supported the FSLN and its Leninist vanguard! So there were two Nicaraguas: a Nicaragua of words, issuing from speeches, slogans, and cooked statistics, and a Nicaragua of wounds and strangled voices, which the world did not hear.

Indeed, the Sandinistas had discovered how censorship can create an "image" desired by the censors. For instance, early in the Reagan administration, Secretary of State Alexander Haig made some ominous threats, saying that the United States could not rule out a naval blockade in Nicaragua. We, in *La Prensa*, consider this threat arrogant and imperialistic, constituting outside intervention in our country's affairs. Violeta and Pedro Joaquín were particularly incensed. But aside from one editorial, the Sandinistas censored our condemnations of external interference in Nicaraguan affairs. Thus they could portray us as "reactionaries," as "traitors to the country," and set us up as ideological straw men to their *ad hominem* attacks, while secretly enjoying the joke. How many *La Prensa* articles and editorials were censored in this manner! And thus, by censoring information they could create a manipulated image: after all, no official "record" existed. It was accusation by coerced silence.

On 19 July, the third anniversary of the revolution, and a day on which the government had confiscated twelve companies, Daniel Ortega asked a crowd if they wanted *La Prensa* confiscated also. We were, by now, accustomed to such threats and intimidations, which we took seriously. It was already notorious that Humberto Ortega, the minister of defense, had declared that if there were ever an invasion, they would hang us from the trees, and *Radio Sandino* had announced that, in such a case, we would be flayed alive and shot through the head. We had all received threatening phone calls at all hours of the day, and it was an open secret that the Sandinistas had a blacklist of those who would be executed in the event of an invasion or a comparable emergency so that there would be no leadership or infrastructure left in a post-Sandinista Nicaragua.

The year 1982 was also when the Sandinistas began systematically censoring the words of our murdered editor Pedro Joaquín Chamorro—whom they had declared "martyr of public liberties" on 21 November 1980 (Decree #566). The title had been given to Pedro by *La Prensa* on the day he was murdered. We soon discovered that the Sandinistas paid only lip service to Pedro's memory. They had been happy to use his name in the insurrection, but his words now displeased their dictatorship—just as they had displeased Somoza's dictatorship.

On 26 May 1982 the censor suppressed the speech Pedro had given at *La Prensa's* fiftieth anniversary celebration in 1976, under (our) title:

"Pedro Joaquín defines *La Prensa*." Pablo Antonio Cuadra then wrote the Government Junta a strong letter of protest, calling attention to the extremes that had been reached in "preventing the publication of one of Pedro Joaquín's writings whose text is fundamental for the veneration of freedom which is essential to the revolution." He added:

> We don't believe that the Emergency Law may at any time envision the abolishment of the progressive, patriotic, and democratic thought of one who has been officially declared by the Revolution: "Martyr of Public Liberties"—and whose death contributed substantially to the liberation of Nicaragua. *La Prensa* is with the Revolution because of this legacy of conduct and thought expressed by Pedro Joaquín Chamorro in the censored speech, and nobody benefits more from those ideals of pluralistic democracy and freedom than the Revolution itself, which has formalized them in its Fundamental Charter. For that reason, we vigorously protest this extraordinary censorship, which, in addition to so many daily restrictions, now has reached the extreme of suppressing Pedro Joaquín's words...We believe that the greater the liberty allowed by the government, the greater the strength and security it reveals to both the Nicaraguan people and the outside world. In this sense, a free press would encourage the Nicaraguan people to have confidence in the Revolution.

The Sandinista censor's reply was unwittingly ironic. Lt. Blandón explained that, "For them," Pedro was "worthy of respect and admiration for his obstinate and unswerving conduct, criticizing and denouncing the abuses of the dynastic power." She concluded that all these merits:

> ...finally led to his sacrifice and the honorable title of Martyr of Public Liberties. Because of that, we cannot be indifferent to the fact that in the paper you edit articles are reproduced which the Martyr wrote on concrete situations that no longer apply in today's Nicaragua, and which if applied to the present moment, would both disorient and confuse the reader and violate the legal measures of the Emergency Decree. In view of the above, it was absolutely imperative for our Office not to authorize the publication, on this date, or at any other, of Dr. Chamorro Cardenal's speech on the fiftieth anniversary of your paper's existence. Revolutionary greetings,

Nelba Cecilia Blandón
Director of Communications Media

La Prensa

In effect, Blandón was the victim of her own contradictions. Thus the "concrete situation that no longer apply in today's Nicaragua" (the Somocista period) "if applied to the present (Sandinista) moment, would disorient and confuse." The Sandinista confusion was clear as was the disorientation, because by May 1982, the Sandinista regime had already surpassed Somoza in censorship and repression, discarding participant pluralism and freedom of the press, as well as basic human rights and civil guarantees. Everything was reduced to militarism and ideology. It was as if the militant extreme right of *Somocismo* joined the militant extreme left of *Sandinismo* in a *reductio ad absurdum* where extremes meet and blend into each other.

Indeed, a distinguished colleague of *La Prensa* brought us an old clipping describing the Nazi system (the regime, without reference to ideology), and the points of coincidence with the Sandinista system were so many that, despite our reproducing it without comment, the censor removed it. Undoubtedly, according to the government, the comparison would "disorient and confuse" our Nicaraguan readers.

Thus it followed that Pedro's speech would also be dangerously confusing, for it defined *La Prensa*'s code of conduct, the thoughts and the ideals we uphold, and our denunciation of censorship and persecution.

In the speech, Pedro said:

> I must speak of the present situation, which is very similar to other situations we have had in the past: a situation of censorship, of persecution, of threats, all within a strategy that denotes the desire or the need of the dictatorial regime to destroy *La Prensa*.... *La Prensa* has been a newspaper with a pluralistic intention, which, as you well know, means: an intention to allow a dialogue with the diverse ideological currents; and besides being pluralistic, to lead —and this is the definitive line of *La Prensa*—to lead towards social progress for the benefit of Nicaragua's marginalized majorities.

In November 1982, we ran a series of interviews with one of the members of the Governing Junta, Dr. Rafael Córdova Rivas. At various points, Dr. Córdova Rivas criticized the government's prior censorship and this was, of course, censored by the censor. On 18 November, 80 percent of our material was censored, and the censor deliberately took seven and a half hours to read two and a half pages. Consequently, we could not publish for that day. On the same day, we then sent a letter to the Governing Junta in which we made the following points:

As you can see, several key paragraphs were deleted from an interview with Governing Junta member Dr. Rafael Córdova Rivas. Among others, the censor removed precisely the paragraph in which Dr. Córdova Rivas had questioned the capacity and good judgement of the censors. The accuracy of his argument was demonstrated by the very fact that the censors dared to censor him: a member of the Governing Junta and therefore much higher in the ranks of government authority than the censors. If we may no longer publish what you yourselves say, in an attempt at constructive criticism that reflects the degree of pluralism existing within the Junta, what then may we publish?

In the same letter, we also made this point:

The censors likewise deleted a special report by a former KGB agent in which he stated that the KGB had advised Soviet President Leonid Brezhnev and the Politburo against invading Afghanistan. The article was duly signed and dealt with a topic that has not the slightest connection with the Nicaraguan State of Emergency, and by no stretch of the imagination could be said to endanger the security of the Nicaraguan nation or to favor aggression against our country.

We received no direct reply or response from the government, but in the Sandinista media, the shrill campaign against *La Prensa* grew even louder. On 20 August the government censored an open letter to the Nicaraguan people by Violeta Chamorro, former member of the Sandinista Junta. It is an appropriate conclusion to the year 1982:

With each passing day, freedom of the press is further limited in our country, not only preventing us from reporting the factual events that occur daily in our social, political, and economic life, but also keeping us from expressing our own opinions, from making editorial comments and, with that, from proclaiming and defending the ideas that served as a banner for *La Prensa* and for the Nicaraguan people to overthrow the Somoza dictatorship.

...Without freedom of the press, there is no representative democracy, no individual liberty, no social justice, no governmental responsibility, and, of course, no distributive justice or equality among citizens; on the contrary, there is darkness, impunity, abuse, mediocrity, and repression.

Who Killed Pedro Joaquín?

WHEN PEDRO JOAQUÍN Chamorro was murdered, most Nicaraguans believed that Somoza was behind the assassination. After all, Pedro had vehemently opposed the Somoza dynasty and had tried to overthrow the Somoza government forcibly on various occasions. Once he had even declared that the FSLN was a movement to overthrow an "illegitimate regime." When Somoza was pressured to lift censorship, Pedro launched sustained, furious attacks against his cronies and him. Because of Pedro's prestige and the volatile political climate of the country, his death ignited the national insurrection that led to Somoza's downfall.

Somoza, of course, insisted that neither he nor anyone else in his government or family was involved in the assassination. He claimed that Luis Pallais Debayle, his cousin and the editor of the family newspaper *Novedades*, came to him shortly after the assassination with a reporter from *Novedades*. The reporter told him that several days before a man had come to the newspaper seeking Pallais. This man was Silvio Peña, and he was married to a sister of the reporter's wife. The reporter asked Peña why he wanted to see Pallais, and he replied that he was seeking a promise of political protection because he intended to kill Pedro Joaquín Chamorro. The reporter told Peña that he was crazy; Luis Pallais would not give political protection for such an act, and he was not even in the country at the time. He dismissed Peña's request as braggadocio.

Immediately after the assassination, all the principal murderers were apprehended. Indeed, the assassination was not done professionally. For instance, the assassins used their own vehicles. The car used to block Pedro's car was quickly identified by witnesses as the getaway car.

Somoza subsequently had Peña detained and subjected to an intense interrogation. Peña quickly confessed that he and two others had been hired by Dr. Pedro Ramos—a Cuban exile and manager of the Plasma Pheresis Centro Americana plant in Managua. *La Prensa* had earlier conducted an investigation of Ramos's blood bank and accused him of buying the blood of impoverished Nicaraguans for $5.25 per pint and selling it abroad for enormous profits.

Ramos had litigation pending against Pedro for defamation of character, but the day before the assassination he left Nicaragua after telling one of the Chamorro family lawyers that he was dropping the suit. The next day, 10 January 1979, Pedro was murdered. Later in Miami, Ramos categorically denied that he was in any way involved in the assassination, and he sent our family a private letter in which he swore before God that he was innocent. We never made the letter public, believing that the ongoing investigations would establish the truth—especially as all the accused assassins had been captured.

Later, Lucrecia del Carmen Castro Barahone, Ramos's secretary, testified that she had given $4,000 to Peña Rivas on behalf of Ramos a few weeks before the murder. She was not closely cross-examined; in addition, her stepfather worked for Somoza's newspaper, *Novedades*. Most people found her an unconvincing witness.

In the meantime, three other men implicated in the murder were also captured. In order to disassociate his government from the assassination, Somoza had the suspects testify on radio and television and made them available for questioning by about fifty members of the press, radio, and television. For three days, Nicaraguans heard the men confess their part in the crime and name names.

Of course, both the brother and the attorney of Silvio Peña insisted he had been forced to "confess" under torture—but this was not convincing. There were, however, a series of anomalies. For instance, all the suspects were captured within a very short period of time. Peña, himself, was picked up at his home, and his car fit the description of the described "get-away" car. This all seemed a little too neat and quick. In addition, the fact that Ramos said he intended to drop the lawsuit on the day before the murder was itself suspicious. And there were other discrepancies and contradictions that bothered us. But there was no doubt that the four men accused by the Somoza government were the murderers of Pedro Joaquín Chamorro—on this everyone agrees. Only the motives and the instigators of the crime remain in doubt.

After passions had cooled, most people in Nicaragua came to believe that Somoza was not directly involved in the assassination but that his oldest son, Anastasio Somoza Portocarrero, might somehow be implicated in it. First, Somoza had always insisted that Pedro Joaquín and *La Prensa* were the best proof that he was not the brutal dictator that his enemies claimed he was. In his last two years in Nicaragua (when censorship was sporadic), Somoza enjoyed showing international visitors the latest *La Prensa* and its attacks against him and his government as demonstrations that there was genuine freedom in Nicaragua. Second, given the fact that he would be the primary suspect if anything happened to Pedro Joaquín, it would have been a colossal error for him to have had Pedro murdered. Somoza was a dictator, but he was not stupid. Pedro alive was, as he said, his "insurance." Indeed, on two different occasions, Somoza emphasized this to both Carlos Andrés Pérez and Rodrigo Carazo Odio, respectively the presidents of Venezuela and Costa Rica.

The Sandinistas also had no love for Pedro. For instance, on 3 November 1975 Carlos Fonseca, the primary founder of the FSLN, wrote that through persons like "Pedro Joaquín Chamorro," the "class enemy," could try to infiltrate or undercut the FSLN by passing themselves off as "Sandinistas," later to create divisions through groups of "democratic Sandinistas." According to Fonseca, Pedro Joaquín "had even dared to exhibit a portrait of Sandino in his office."* Fonseca insisted that "elements of the enemy" deserve death but that the general interests of the FSLN did not, at that time, permit such deaths to be realized. He emphasized, however, that it was important to promote the appropriate political atmosphere in order to create the belief "that the popular masses themselves are the ones that turn more and more against [Somoza's] tyranny and that there is no conspiracy by a certain group of people" [read the Sandinistas]. He thus stressed the importance of emphasizing "political convenience" through actions that contribute to the Sandinista struggle. Fonseca concluded that if assassinations were necessary, the concrete circumstances would dictate how they would be done. [*Bajo la bandera del Sandinismo*, (Managua: Editorial Nueva Nicaragua) 1985, pp. 174, 178-179.]

---

* Ironically, the photograph of Sandino that Fonseca mentioned was the first and only portrait, for some time, to be exhibited in the Government House after 19 July 1979. As nobody at that time had a portrait of Sandino, Violeta Chamorro removed it from Pedro's office to her own Government Junta office.

As late as 27 September 1986 the Sandinista government, through its embassy in Guatemala, replied to an article by Violeta Chamorro, in which she protested the 26 June closing of *La Prensa*. The embassy declared that in the 1970s, American imperialism had realized that Somoza's usefulness was over and had hoped to cultivate Pedro Joaquín as the next imperialist agent. The Sandinistas hence saw Pedro as a prominent member of the hated bourgeoisie—a class enemy who threatened their position in post-Somoza Nicaragua. For instance, in the 1970s Pedro had formed a new political coalition composed of an alliance of anti-Somoza parties and two unions representing all ideologies—from right to left, with the exception of both the Somocistas and the Sandinistas. The new coalition was called The Democratic Union for Liberation (UDEL), and the Sandinistas feared that Pedro and UDEL would fill any political vacuum left by Somoza—especially as Pedro's popularity and prestige made him a logical alternative to both the Sandinistas and the Somocistas. In 1977, the Sandinistas denounced UDEL as a "bourgeois" organization. During the last meeting organized by UDEL in Chinandega in November 1977, they infiltrated it in order to disrupt the proceedings.

Of course, Pedro had no illusions about the Sandinistas. He knew they were Marxist-Leninists; thus in *La Prensa* he emphasized that Sandino was a nationalist and not a Communist, as the Sandinistas suggested. When the Sandinistas took power, they censored this article when we tried to run it again in *La Prensa*. (See Appendix B.) Pedro also emphatically criticized the regime of Fidel Castro—a regime and a dictator that the Sandinistas enthusiastically admired. In his last article on 6 January 1978 before he was assassinated, he took exception to the way the word "bourgeois" was being abused by various forces in Nicaragua—pointing out that the "bourgeoisie" comprised a large part of the Nicaraguan population.

On 27 August 1979, shortly after the Sandinistas took power, Sandinista Judge Víctor Manuel Ordóñez annulled the Somoza government's judicial investigation of Pedro's death. On 6 September Tomás Borge, the minister of interior, announced that he was personally in charge of the new investigation and would soon obtain "the full truth" from the prisoners.

On 27 September, Judge Ordóñez sent an urgent note to Borge, asking him where the accused prisoners could be located. The chief of police had told Ordóñez that the prisoners could not be found in any of the country's jails. Sergio Ramírez, a member of the ruling Junta, announced two days later in New York that two of the prisoners had escaped from jail during the chaos of Somoza's last days but that they had been recaptured. In fact, one fugitive, Silvio Vega Zúñiga, had escaped to Costa Rica and was living there.

Indeed, when most of Somoza's National Guardsmen had fled on 19 July 1979, the inmates at the Tipitapa jail in Managua, left unguarded, had escaped. The killers of Pedro Joaquín, however, were spotted by many people before they were recaptured by Marcel Pallais, a young Sandinista officer who was a nephew of Luis Pallais, ex-editor of *Novedades*. Marcel Pallais was subsequently murdered under circumstances that remain unclear. The only thing that has been established is that his body was dumped on a Managua street on 5 October 1979. He had been shot through the head. The Sandinistas immediately declared that "supporters of deposed President Anastasio Somoza had committed the murder." They provided no names.

Several weeks later, Tomás Borge, the minister of interior, changed the official line, asserting on Sandinista TV that he had captured "the band of common criminals" who had murdered Marcel Pallais. Borge, again, furnished no names or details.

In the meantime, Borge had held a press conference on 9 October to announce that Anastasio Somoza Portocarrero, Somoza's eldest son, had killed Pedro Joaquín Chamorro. On 15 October, Judge Ordóñez formally indicted Somoza, his son, and Fausto Zelaya Centeno, an ex-minister of housing in the Somoza government, for the murder of Pedro Joaquín. He then called on Borge to testify.

Borge appeared in court on 25 October and testified that "comrades Marcel and Gabriel" (pseudonyms) had interrogated the prisoners charged with Chamorro's murder and had "convinced" them of the need to tell the truth. Borge claimed that the "truth" extracted from the prisoners proved that Somoza's son had murdered Chamorro. Borge didn't explain how they had been convinced to tell the truth, and the judge did not follow up with any pertinent questions.

In January 1980 the prisoners appeared in court. One of them, Silvio Peña, told the judge how Somoza's son had personally shot Pedro Joaquín with two pistols. As Pedro had been murdered with shotguns, there was a dramatic silence in the court—Peña's account was obviously absurd. Realizing that his story didn't fit the facts, Peña then said he wanted to clarify his last statement. He declared that the pistols were long—roughly measuring from his elbow to his fingertips and that they were double-barreled. (He was either lying to deceive or lying to emphasize the absurdity of his confession.) Indeed, his testimony was so absurd and contrived that we, at *La Prensa*, declared that such lies were revolting. (*La Prensa*, 17 January 1980, p. 1; 18 January 1980, p. 1) This in itself was significant, given that *La Prensa*, at this time, was still under the control of the Sandinistas within *La Prensa* and that the prisoners were Comandante Borge's star witnesses.

Because Violeta and the Chamorro family had not previously retained any lawyer—alleging that the Somoza regime was responsible for Pedro's murder—the judicial proceedings were conducted by the state, even after the Sandinistas took power.

By 1981, however, the defendants had still not been tried by the Sandinista government; consequently, Violeta and the family decided to retain their own lawyers in order to speed up the process and bring the case before a jury. But before the jury was impanelled and the trial initiated (presided over by Judge Félix Trejos y Trejos), Dr. Ernesto Castillo Martínez, the minister of justice, (subsequently ambassador to the Soviet Union) and one of the FSLN's most important ideologues, requested that he, in behalf of the revolutionary government, be the principal prosecutor, in collaboration with our family's lawyers.

The jury was finally impanelled on 9 June 1981, at the urging of our lawyers, José Antonio Tejerino Medrano and his staff. During the trial there was public speculation that Silvio Peña, the principal defendant who had elected to defend himself, intended to announce that the Sandinistas had planned the assassination of Pedro Joaquín. Indeed, Peña had "promised" that he would reveal "surprises" (*La Prensa,* 10 June 1981, p. 12).

In the Nicaraguan court system, the prosecution makes its case first, and then either the lawyer(s) or the defendant, in this case Silvio Peña, responds. In turn, the prosecution customarily responds to the defense, in which case the latter has the right to speak again. This is what almost always happens. But if the prosecution does not respond, the trial is immediately ended.

In the first round—the trial lasted twenty-six hours with three recesses—Silvio Peña said nothing about any Sandinista involvement in Pedro Joaquín's murder. At this point, the family lawyers had to decide if they would respond to Peña. Ernesto Castillo, as principal prosecutor, had a meeting with Violeta and the lawyers and told them that he did not consider it advisable to allow Peña to speak again. The lawyers complied with his request.

I did not attend this meeting and thus I was surprised when, on the same day (10 June), the judge announced that the trial was over and the jury would retire to deliberate its verdict. Silvio Peña was also surprised and protested to the judge, requesting that he be allowed to speak, but the judge denied his request.

Some time after, Dr. Tijerino, the chief family lawyer, told me that he and his staff had made an error in not allowing Peña to speak—but at the time they thought that he would accuse the Sandinistas of Pedro's murder—a charge that seemed without substance and one that would have disrupted the proceedings. (Ironically, in January 1988 Ernesto Castillo was accused of being involved in Pedro's assassination in an investigatory article published in *La República,* one of Costa Rica's principal newspapers.)

On 18 June, "three years, five months, and eight days after the murder," the judge sentenced the convicts (seven of whom were in jail and two at large) to prison terms ranging from eighteen years to the maximum of thirty years.

On 9 February 1983 Violeta de Chamorro appeared before the vice-minister of justice and insisted that the legal case against those responsible for her husband's death (those who originally plotted the murder) be pursued and that those responsible be extradited to Nicaragua—as had been promised to her many times by various comandantes of the revolution. Her visit to the vice-minister was partially censored in *La Prensa,* particularly her questions about why the government had not followed up and extradited the accused. When nothing happened, on 16 February she wrote a letter to the members of the Governing Junta protesting the censorship of her husband's words in *La Prensa*—a censorship more severe than the censorship during the "fatal days of the Somoza dynasty." Violeta again insisted that the comandantes carry out the legal process and the extradition of those who had planned her husband's murder. She told the comandantes that she didn't think the government had the least interest in pursuing this and that the Sandinista courts had not discovered one thing that the Somocista courts had not previously established. (See Appendix C.)

In addition to all the irregularities, Violeta noted that the Sandinistas showed surprising intransigence during the preliminary investigation of the captured suspects. For instance, the Sandinista comandantes denied the Chamorro family permission to hire an independent investigator to question the alleged killers. Violeta says that they told her that "we could not question the suspects because they [the Sandinistas] were going to do it. So far, they have done nothing more. Why didn't they allow the suspects to testify [to an independent investigator] and why didn't they conduct a good trial? Many believe that it is because the Sandinistas themselves are involved."* In addition, a few months after the Sandinista triumph, Tomás Borge came to Violeta's home and proposed that he would kill the suspects in order to finish the case. Violeta was horrified and told Borge that there must be a trial and that the prisoners must not be murdered. Moreover, the Sandinistas cancelled the extradition proceedings of Silvio Vega Zúñiga, who had escaped from prison on 19 July 1979, fled to Costa Rica, and had been convicted of Pedro Joaquín's murder *in absentia*.

On the eve of 10 January 1982 Pedro Joaquín Chamorro Barrios, the eldest son of Pedro Joaquín, received a collect call from someone he has agreed not to identify. The caller said that Vega Zúñiga was living in the village of Barranca, Costa Rica. Pedro agreed to pay a reward if the caller's information led to Vega's capture. He was then given Vega's address in Costa Rica. As relations between the Sandinista government and *La Prensa* were strained, Pedro figured that this was a matter on which both could agree. He assumed that the government would want Silvio Vega extradited to Nicaragua to quell rumors about Sandinista complicity in his father's death.

I personally went to Costa Rica to see if it were possible to have Vega arrested and extradited to Nicaragua. But the Costa Rican authorities informed me that as Vega had not committed a crime in Costa Rica, he could not be arrested. He could be extradited, however, if the proper extradition procedures were put in motion in Nicaragua, in which case they would be happy to collaborate with us in having Vega extradited to Nicaragua.

Pedro Joaquín then discussed the matter with Dr. Roberto Argüello Hurtado, the Supreme Court chief justice and a good friend of Pedro's murdered father. Argüello was very interested in the details and, upon learning the address, promised that he would immediately start proceedings for the recapture and extradition of Silvio Vega. But months went by without any word from Argüello. Consequently, Pedro returned to inquire about the course of the investigation, assuming by this time that Silvio Vega would have been apprehended in Costa Rica. Dr. Argüello's

---

* Interview in the Los Angeles newspaper *La Opinión*, 7 May 1985, p. 6.

response startled him: "Look, Pedro, the extradition papers were lost at the Ministry of Interior."

There were many anomalies. The extradition papers were prepared by a judge and sent to the Supreme Court and then to the Ministry of Interior instead of the Ministry of Foreign Relations, which should have then sent the papers to the Costa Rican Ministry of Foreign Relations. Moreover, if the papers for extradition were lost, then the logical response would have been to have asked the judge for a new set of papers. Why didn't Argüello Hurtado do this if the Sandinista government was truly interested in extraditing Vega? Indeed, we found it extremely puzzling that the Ministry of Interior, always so efficient and methodical, could have casually misplaced the papers for the capture and extradition of one of Pedro Joaquín Chamorro's assassins.

The Sandinistas did nothing. In 1985, Silvio Vega was arrested by the Costa Rican police for participating in a street fight. But it was only after Claudia Chamorro, the Nicaraguan ambassador to Costa Rica and the daughter of Pedro Joaquín and Violeta, discovered that Vega was in jail and had then formally requested and put in motion the machinery for extradition, that the Sandinistas, six years after the fact, hypocritically called for Vega's extradition.

In Managua, the Sandinista press, particularly *El Nuevo Diario*, joined in the hypocrisy with calls for "justice." *El Nuevo Diario* mendaciously published an article linking Vega with the Contras and declaring that Vega's extradition had not been expedited because of his links with ex-members of Somoza's National Guard and that all these sinister forces had protected him in Costa Rica. The Sandinista newspaper even tried to imply illogically that Pedro Joaquín Chamorro Barrios was an accomplice in the "impunity" enjoyed by his father's assassin because the Costa Rican newspaper *La Nación*, in which Pedro published a weekly anti-Sandinista supplement, had also published an interview with Silvio Vega. The article ended cynically, affirming that "the revolutionary government has put forth its best legal and diplomatic efforts to ensure that the criminal obtains his just punishment." I wrote to Xavier Chamorro, editor of *El Nuevo Diario*, defending Pedro and reminding Xavier that the Sandinista government was responsible for Vega's impunity, not the counterrevolution. My letter was censored in *La Prensa* and, not surprisingly, it did not appear in *El Nuevo Diario*.

Disillusioned with Sandinista stonewalling in the case of her husband's death, Violeta de Chamorro wrote a letter dated 5 May 1986 to the Costa

Rican minister of foreign relations asking him not to extradite Vega to Nicaragua. (Under Costa Rican law, Vega must first serve a two-year sentence before he can be extradited.) Violeta pointed out that this would leave Vega in the hands of a government she had no confidence in and that she would prefer it if the investigation were carried out in Costa Rica because conditions for justice did not exist in Nicaragua.

In January 1988, however, Vega was extradited to Nicaragua, and I was able to see him on 19 January, after I was briefly imprisoned and interrogated on my return from a trip to Guatemala. During my imprisonment, Lenín Cerna, chief of state security, told me that the Sandinistas had discovered that Pedro's assassination was planned by *"el Chigüín"* (Somoza Debayles's son). The dialogue then continued as follows:

"I see no real proof of this. That is what has been said, but nobody has shown any real proof," I replied.

"What do you want, that I bring you Silvio Vega? Well I have him, I am going to leave him here with you so that he can tell you everything. I'll bring him to you now...bring Silvio Vega here!" Cerna shouted. All those who accompanied him started to run. There were a few moments of expectation. "What's the matter?" demanded Cerna. We heard some metal doors being opened and suddenly a man came running, bent and with his hands behind his back. He was bearded and balding, with his remaining hair a mess. They pushed him against the wall.

"Who killed Pedro?" Cerna shouted.

With his eyes still looking towards the floor, the man began talking in a tremulous voice. "I do not deny it, I participated. I was driving the car with Acevedo in it, but I did not want any part of it. When they killed him I turned away, I did not want to see. Acevedo was in the rear seat, and he was carrying a shotgun covered by a cloth. I do not know if it was a twelve or twenty gauge. I don't know, they forced me. I did not want to."

"Who forced you?" asked Cerna.

"Well...it was..."

"Wasn't it Bermudez?" interrupted Cerna.

"Yes, yes, that's it...it was Bermudez."

"Which Bermudez?" asked Cerna.

"Well, I don't know, it was a Bermudez," said Vega.

"Wasn't it that Bermudez who killed people in Matagalpa, one of Somoza's generals who dedicated himself to killing people in Matagalpa?" Cerna reminded him.

"Ah...yes...that's him, the one from Matagalpa."
"But who ordered that Pedro should be killed?" Cerna asked.
"It was Somoza!" said Vega, moving his hands from behind him.
"Which Somoza?" asked Cerna.
"The old Somoza!" said Vega (obviously referring to Somoza Debayle).

The dialogue was suddenly cut off because Vega had obviously not pleased Cerna, and today we remain convinced that the material killers were and are ignorant of who really planned Pedro's assassination.

One final detail: Humberto de la Concepción Granados Ordóñez, who was sentenced to eighteen years in prison on 17 June 1981 for providing weapons to Pedro Joaquín's assassins, was subsequently released quietly. In March 1986, he was arrested again for another murder and then released again.

On the basis of these and other details, we are left with questions, doubts, and suspicions. Somoza certainly had a conspicuous motive for murdering Pedro Joaquín, as did the Sandinistas who could at once get rid of a despised "class" rival and pin the blame on a repudiated dictator. The latter gives us pause: after all, the only ones who benefited from Pedro's death were the Sandinistas themselves.

Censorship, the Church, and *Vende Patrias*

IN 1983 *La Prensa* was unable to publish for eight days due to excessive prior censorship and for one day because the Sandinistas closed it. Excessive censorship kept us from publishing on 3 May, 12 July, and 12 August. The censored material for the 12 August issue concerned the government's denial of a salary increase. On 23 August the primary news related to a communiqué from the papal nuncio; again we could not publish because of excessive censorship. When the principal news of 31 August dealt with the Nicaraguan Bishops' pastoral letter on mandatory military service, it was the same story, and again on 4 and 5 October. And finally, on 2 November, we could not publish because the news dealt with the Curia's protest of *turba* attacks on churches the Sunday before.

In October 1983 unidentified attackers fired a rocket at *La Prensa*'s printing plant, but fortunately it missed. We had no doubt who was behind the attack.

The following day the Kissinger Commission arrived in Managua, and we had a meeting with it that included Pedro Joaquín Barrios, Roberto Cardenal, and myself. Since the rocket attack had happened recently, Pedro told Kissinger about it, and Kissinger smiled and replied: "How I would have liked to have fired a rocket at the *Washington Post!*"

Although we had no doubts about who was behind the attack, the investigation by the Sandinista police was pure theater. They appeared and took the pick-up truck of Carlos Holmann (one of *La Prensa*'s board of directors) after their police dogs had begun sniffing it. The police, of course, did not accuse Holmann, and of course they never found out who fired the rocket.

On the night of 27 October Luis Mora Sánchez, a correspondent, was stopped by a Sandinista soldier and asked for identification papers. When the soldier saw where Mora worked, he exclaimed, "a live one from *La Prensa!*" He then called his superior officer and Mora was taken to the *Zona Franca*, a prison near the Augusto César Sandino airport. As he had done nothing wrong and his papers were in order, Mora expected to be released shortly. But that same night he was told by the military prosecutor, Lolo Juárez, that he would be imprisoned three days for "being with *La Prensa*." The next day, however, the prosecutor showed him a typewritten paper sentencing him to sixty days in prison for "disrespect to authority." Mora was later released.

His first-person account was censored from *La Prensa* on 15 November 1983. Other articles that were censored in a three-day period, between 15 and 18 November, include the following: a plea from the Center of Nicaraguan Workers (an independent union) that the government stop harassing its members, a plea from members of the Indian community of Jinotega for land to work on—their land had been confiscated; an article about the arrival of an Italian ship that unloaded diesel and gasoline supplies in the port of Corinto and an article about the Independent Liberal Party's intention to ask that the traditional December bonus given to Nicaraguan workers be restored.

A highly notorious closing was to occur on 14 August. On the night of 11 August, Sandinista mobs stoned the house of Violeta Barrios de Chamorro—the widow of Pedro Joaquín and former member of the Revolutionary Junta. We submitted to the censor a note that we intended to publish, but it was censored. In the note, we briefly related the facts, characterized the act as "cowardly," and pointed out that Violeta's house had been desecrated before. We made no accusations or insinuations as to who did it. We were hence outraged that a brief note of thirteen lines was censored for no legitimate reason, but then again we were outraged daily by the Sandinistas' ubiquitous censorship. This time, however, Violeta told us to go ahead and publish the note on 13 August. As a result, the Ministry of Interior prohibited us from publishing the following day, 14 August.

During *La Prensa's* seven-year existence under the Sandinistas, we sometimes submitted material to prior censorship, knowing that it would be censored. We did this for one primary reason: we wanted to record our moral struggle against the dictatorship; even if it couldn't be published in Nicaragua, we wanted a record of our protest against the Sandinista state's multitudinous oppressions. For a while, we were able to distribute these censored articles to foreign embassies (including the Soviet) so that somewhere our voices could be heard above the orchestrated chants and slogans of the Sandinista propaganda machine. Hence we would continue to document specific acts of oppression; we continued writing our articles and editorials, knowing that we were, in effect, writing primarily for the censor. But in a larger sense, we were also writing for our collective conscience and for a people who had no voice. We were writing for Nicaragua. If our words reached one diplomat, one reporter, then we had succeeded in being a voice, however precarious and tiny, for those who had no voice.

There were specific prohibited subjects that we always submitted to prior censorship, such as the desperate pleas of mothers and families of the thousands of prisoners abused and tortured in Sandinista jails and prisons. Everyone in Nicaragua knows someone who is suffering in those jails and prisons.

And everyone knew (even though we had no "Ava Gardner") that *La Prensa* was censored. And what wasn't censored? A photo of an elephant on water skis: prohibited for "ideological diversionism." Reports on the Soviets in Afghanistan, the Cubans in Angola, buses without doors: prohibited. In addition, we were often prohibited from publishing the very things that appeared in *Barricada* and *El Nuevo Diario*, and yet the Sandinistas continued the shameless farce that these papers were also under censorship, "just like *La Prensa*."

During this time, the church was also being systematically censored, not only in its own media, but in *La Prensa* as well. The following examples comprise a small selection of this censorship in *La Prensa*. (This section on the church was written in 1986 by Roberto Cardenal, assistant to the editor of *La Prensa* and secretary of the editorial staff.)

In July 1981, the Sandinistas censored the church for the first time when they cancelled the televised Mass of the archbishop of Managua, Miguel Obando y Bravo. The archbishop had celebrated the Sunday Mass for years on television—the government arbitrarily decided that priests of the so-called "popular church" should also celebrate Mass on television—thus the government injected itself into church affairs. The church rejected the government's interference, and the Sunday Mass disappeared.

In the same month, many religious billboards placed around Managua by groups of Catholics were defaced or destroyed. When we published photographs of the defaced billboards in *La Prensa*, the Sandinistas closed the newspaper for the first time on 10 July. We could not publish for two days.

In August 1981 *La Prensa* published statements made by Fr. Miguel D'Escoto, minister of foreign affairs, reported by United Press International (UPI) and other news agencies. In his statements, D'Escoto accused Archbishop Obando of being the primary instigator of the counterrevolution. The Sandinista government denied that D'Escoto had said any such thing, and on 19 August, they closed *La Prensa* for three days. To no avail, we established that D'Escoto had indeed made the statement reported by foreign news agencies.

On 15 March 1982 the Sandinistas declared a state of emergency. They established prior censorship and used it as a weapon to silence the church, while they simultaneously strengthened the "popular church." For instance, in July 1982 the Nicaraguan hierarchy decided to transfer Fr. Arias Caldera to another parish in Nicaragua. Fr. Arias already had two churches and as one was needed for a newly ordained priest, this was a simple administrative move. But because Fr. Arias also happened to be a Sandinista sympathizer (he had also been a Somoza sympathizer), the Sandinista media turned the transfer into a political event that they exploited for propaganda purposes.

Barricada, the official newspaper of the FSLN, published seventeen front-page articles, and *El Nuevo Diario* published another seventeen articles. In contrast, *La Prensa* was censored dozens of times. In addition, the Sandinistas attempted to use this manufactured *cause célèbre* to convert Fr. Arias into a substantial rival of Archbishop Obando. They presented Fr. Arias as "the archbishop of the poor" in order to celebrate him as the archbishop of "the people." Father Arias was suddenly invited to state ceremonies where he supposedly represented the church. Even today he appears before and after the televised Sandinista news program *Noticiero Sandinista*. But despite the Sandinistas' endeavors, he never supplanted Archbishop Obando in the hearts and minds of the people.

On 7 August 1981 *La Prensa* attempted to publish a letter from Pope John Paul II to the Nicaraguan bishops. In the letter, the Pope condemned the popular church, and he urged religious obedience to the bishops in the spirit of Christian unity. The Pope's letter was censored. On 8 August we tried again to publish it, but the letter was censored again. On Monday, 9 August, the same letter under the title of "Applause for the Pope in the Churches," accompanied by commentaries from people who had heard the letter read from the pulpits on Sunday, was censored for the third time. Consequently, as a protest against the state censorship of the Pope's letter, we did not publish on this day. On 10 August the Sandinistas finally permitted the letter to be published one time only in all the newspapers. But there was a Sandinista catch: the letter was to be accompanied with an insulting communiqué from the Sandinista censor, mendaciously accusing the Pope of not having condemned a Contra "massacre" that had occurred after the letter had been written. Needless to say, the communiqué had nothing to do with the contents of the Pope's letter.

The censor insisted that the government communiqué should precede the Pope's letter, but we refused to publish it in this form. Because it was, however, important to get the Pope's letter in print, we agreed that if the letter appeared on the front page as principal news, then the communiqué could appear in another place. The Sandinistas' response was to censor us again on 11 August; consequently, we refused to publish for a second time. On 12 August, the censor ordered us to print the letter and communiqué in the form they wanted, but we refused and, for the third time in protest, *La Prensa* did not appear. On 13 August we again sent the letter and the Sandinista communiqué, appearing below the letter, to the censor's office. This time the censor (Lt. Nelba Blandón) approved them, but she censored another article titled *"La Prensa* Explains Why It Wasn't Published on Wednesday and Thursday."

The Pope was, in a sense, censored again in regard to his forthcoming visit to Nicaragua (4 March 1983). We could not announce the Pope's visit, because the Sandinistas insisted that only they should officially announce both the invitation and the Pope's acceptance. But there was more to the censorship than this. In fact, from the middle of December 1982 until February 1983, the Pope's name could not be mentioned at all. This included any news or commentary dealing with the Bulgarian connection to the attempt on his life and any pastoral visits and declarations made by the Pope in Central American countries. During this period, John Paul's name could not appear at all in *La Prensa*.

After 7 February 1983 the government announced the Pope's visit, but it continued to censor various news items selectively, especially those referring to the visit as a pastoral trip of a religious leader rather than a visit from a head of state. After 4 March, the day of the Pope's visit, the government censored any criticism of its organized disruption of the Pope's Mass and the profanation of the Eucharist. The censorship included letters, commentaries, and vindications of the Pope. During this period, more than 500 news items and commentaries referring to the Pope were censored.

On 5 April 1984 the Nicaraguan Catholic church asked the Ministry of Interior for permission to transmit the liturgical events of Holy Week without censorship. This was censored in *La Prensa* on 6 April.

On 26 April 1984 the Episcopal Conference of Nicaraguan Bishops released a pastoral letter on pardon and reconciliation as a formula for ending the war. In response, the Sandinista media polemically attacked the bishops, but the bishops were not permitted to defend themselves in *La Prensa* or elsewhere. *Barricada*, the official newspaper of the FSLN, published sixty-seven articles and the equivalent of ten pages of cartoons and drawings that ridiculed and insulted the bishops, especially Archbishop Obando. Anything that we tried to publish in defense of the bishops was censored.

On 10 July 1984 the Sandinista government arbitrarily expelled ten foreign priests from the country. Every time we tried to publish this fact, the government censored us. Thus anyone interested in the expulsions will not find anything mentioned in *La Prensa*. The same day, *La Prensa* was again not published. As the principal news of the day related to the expulsions, there were not sufficient materials left to fill up the spaces emptied by the censor.

In the first days of October 1985, more than thirty foreign priests from the diocese of Granada were called by Immigration and threatened with expulsion if they involved themselves in politics. In addition, seminarians from the dioceses of Chontales and Granada were drafted into the army—despite a previous agreement between the government and church that seminarians would not be drafted. Consequently, the Nicaraguan bishops sent President Daniel Ortega a telegram saying that they felt that the government wanted to intimidate the church and that the threats from Immigration reminded them of the expulsion of the ten priests in July 1984. The telegram was censored in *La Prensa*.

On 8 October, the Sandinista government censored a series of archdiocesan news items taken from the Catholic church's Sunday bulletin. One of the items announced the publication of a Catholic newspaper called *Iglesia*. On 12 October the Sandinistas confiscated the first edition of *Iglesia* (10,000 copies) as well as the church's printing press (donated by the West German bishops), and the land, offices, and everything else pertaining to the church's social welfare agency, COPROSA.

On 15 October the Sandinistas declared another state of emergency, and censorship of the church reached higher and more repressive levels. During this time, the Sandinistas utilized prison terms, long interrogations, and psychological and physical torture to terrify the priests and laity who worked for the church hierarchy. Norman Talavera, a *La Prensa* reporter who covered church activities and collaborated in the publication of church materials, was imprisoned for seven days. The Sandinistas tried to pressure him to stop covering church activities.

On 21 October, while visiting Estelí, Cardinal Obando read a communiqué from the Nicaraguan bishops, noting that the church could now only speak from the pulpit—as it had been censored in all the existing media. The Catholic bishops accused the government of intimidating priests, pressuring church laity, and destroying church property. Needless to say, the communiqué was censored and the true meaning lost.

On 1 January 1986, the Sandinista government indefinitely closed *Radio Católica*, leaving the church without a single means of communication. The pretext was that *Radio Católica* had failed to link up with a national network at a prescribed time. All the time the church was being repressed and silenced, it was simultaneously prevented from protesting the government's persecution in the Nicaraguan media. The church could not denounce the systematic censorship, the confiscation of its social welfare offices, and the constant threats and harassment of bishops, priests, and clergy.

On 14 February 1986 Fr. Miguel D'Escoto, the Sandinista minister of foreign affairs, began a much-publicized journey, stopping at fourteen "Stations of the Cross" located throughout the country. At each station, D'Escoto vehemently attacked the bishops, and he particularly targeted Cardinal Obando in a ploy to encourage religious disobedience. On 28 February, in Managua, D'Escoto publicly launched a personal attack on Cardinal Obando, which for sheer disrespect was unprecedented in Nicaragua. D'Escoto's diatribe was taped and shown on Sandinista television on 3 March. Because D'Escoto's remarks were not reported by most of the international media, we have included some of his more revealing comments:

> That poor human being born in Nicaragua and ordained to the priesthood, Miguel Obando, tells the legislators: "Don't worry, because I, I am Cardinal, and I cannot condemn aggression!"
> Could there ever be a more abominable sin in the history of

humanity? I believe, dear brethren, that there is no word uttered by human mouth, no adjective that we could use to truly describe the horror, the disgust produced by this brother of ours...

If you are at your television or radio, don't turn it off! Don't turn it off, Miguel Obando!

The Lord through His humble people—the peasants who suffer the aggression of which you have been the principal accomplice —that God, the God of life, the God of love, of justice but also of mercy, Miguel Obando, has had mercy on you, and that is why He has convoked these people at this moment...

The Lord, therefore, is giving you an opportunity. Meanwhile, and listen carefully: In the name of God and with the authority that comes from God, we tell you that you must immediately abstain from again celebrating the Holy Sacrifice of the Mass. Because the Sacrifice celebrated by the accomplice in the murder of his people is a sacrilegious sacrifice which deeply offends the faith of our people!

There are many more things that we have to tell you, but we will seek a more propitious moment in the next few days.

We warn you beforehand, Miguel Obando y Bravo, not to leave Nicaragua to attend any meeting or conference, for the fate of your immortal soul depends on this!

Listen to the God that is now speaking to you from here! There is nobody in the Vatican nor in Brazil, wherever you may go, wherever it may be, no one who could be more important! And we are going to tell you, not to beg you, but to demand *a dialogue with you!* And this time you are going to grant it in the name of God who gives you the opportunity to repent, to abandon the prepotency, the arrogance, that are characteristics of the God you have been serving but which have nothing to do with the God adored by our people, God the Father of our Lord Jesus Christ!

In an allusion to D'Escoto, the Conference of Bishops tried in vain to publish a communiqué lamenting the unprecedented, calumnious attack by "ecclesiastics who find themselves in an irregular situation with the church." (Because he has refused to resign his governmental position, D'Escoto cannot celebrate Mass.) The communiqué also asked the government to clarify if D'Escoto had made his declarations as a private citizen or as a spokesman for the government. It added that such pronouncements placed these ecclesiastics outside the church in their attempt to encourage the faithful not to obey their legitimate pastors and that it seemed to the bishops that this was a strategy to divide the church and distract the people from the real problems of violence, hunger, and insecurity. But the censor again denied the church's right of defense and censored everything that alluded to D'Escoto's actions and comments.

Here are some of the titles that were censored in *La Prensa*: "D'Escoto Offends the Cardinal"; "Cardinal Obando Pardons Those Who Have Injured Him"; "By Their Fruits You Shall Know Them"; "D'Escoto, Official Voice?"; "Church Awaits Decision on COPROSA and *Radio Católica*"; "Social Democratic Party Condemns D'Escoto's Attack on the Cardinal"; "Cardinal: We Pray For Those Who Offend Us"; "Cardinal Describes Tense Church-State Relations"; "*L'Osservatore Romano* Makes a Declaration on the Stations of the Cross"; "Editorial of *La Nación* [a respected Costa Rican newspaper]: A Martyr of the Church"; "The Liberation of Man Should be Total"; "At the Foot of the Cross My Enemy Becomes My Brother." Moreover, the state censorship of the church and the Cardinal is increasing daily. The Cardinal's homily, published each Sunday in *La Prensa* for the past six years, has been systematically censored since 5 April 1986.

On 8 April 1986 a pastoral letter written by the Nicaraguan bishops on the Eucharist was censored in *La Prensa* and totally ignored by the government media. During Holy Week, a great number of articles about Easter Week were censored, especially the Cardinal's sermons. In addition, the Sandinistas have prohibited the publication of the Sunday church bulletin that appears in all the churches of the world, so that the congregation can follow the readings of the day's Mass. Likewise, all the activities of the Cardinal, who regularly visits towns and rural chapels, are completely censored.

In short, the Sandinistas have systematically censored the church in order to intimidate and silence her.

2.

Censorship of *La Prensa* was always contrived. To justify their policy, the Sandinistas first claimed that censorship applied only to information or news pertaining to national security; later, they justified it on the grounds that there was a state of war. But these excuses and pretexts were a form of juridical propaganda aimed at the outside world. Inside Nicaragua the people knew differently. The Nicaraguan people knew that the censored material had nothing to do with "national security" and that it was being kept from the public because it took issue with the regime's politics, its system of one-party government, its corruption (embezzlement, misappropriation of public funds, large-scale waste), and its creation of a monstrous bureaucracy to implement the dictates of an emerging octopus state. They knew further that it was not just political and administrative affairs that were subject to censorship but all expressions of popular protest, all forms of pluralistic activity, all references to the endeavors of the Catholic Church, and all incidents of natural disasters such as floods and bad harvests.

Now and then the government ended up censoring itself. One such case was an interview given by Captain Nelba Blandón, the government censor, to Eloy O. Aguilar of the Associated Press. In the interview, Captain Blandón defended censorship as "an instrument for defending the revolution" and declared that while some people abroad might not understand it, the Sandinistas were not going to let the press be used as a tool for "destabilizing society." Since *La Prensa* subscribed to the AP wire service, we tried to publish the interview, but Captain Blandón deleted it. When Aguilar returned to Nicaragua, he asked Captain Blandón why she had, in effect, censored her own remarks. Her reply was revealingly totalitarian: "Because the statements I gave you were for publication outside the country, not for here in Nicaragua." As an old Nicaraguan proverb puts it: "Light outside and darkness in your house."

The *Facultad de Ciencias de la Comunicación* of the Sandinista-dominated National Autonomous University of Nicaragua (UNAN) publishes a magazine called *Cuadernos de Periodismo (Journalistic Notebooks)*. In issue number 1, volume 1 of 1983, a Mexican internationalist, Ana Corina Fernández, a psychology professor at UNAN, wrote an article entitled: "Censorship: A Way of Resisting the Ideological Penetration of the Enemy." Such tendentious rationalization is common in Sandinista Nicaragua, where ideas are feared and the "enemy" is everyone who doesn't enthusiastically support the Sandinista state.

In 1983, the government took the following actions to further debilitate *La Prensa:*

1. Starting in 1982 and through part of 1983, it refused to sell us the necessary foreign currency to pay for the imported raw materials without which *La Prensa* cannot operate. The government's strategy was, of course, twofold: it would either run us out of business or make us dependent on them, in a manner similar to the way the ruling party of Mexico (PRI) controls the raw materials and hence many of the newspapers.

2. We were ordered to cut our editions to twelve pages.

3. The government, which controls the transfer of funds in and out of the country through the Central Bank of Managua, intentionally did not pay $75,000 owed by *La Prensa* to a New York paper company and deposited in the Central Bank. The company, which had supplied *La Prensa* with newsprint for thirty years, consequently suspended all shipments of paper. This effectively made us dependent on the government for our paper supply.

4. Consequently, we were forced to cut the run of our daily editions by 20,000 copies.

By the end of 1983, Tomás Borge was justifying Sandinista censorship as an instrument that perpetuates the state's "truth" and prohibits counterrevolutionary "lies." After all, he told anyone who would listen that there was a CIA agent inside *La Prensa* advising us what to publish. And as always, Borge would provide no specifics. But it wasn't necessary. The labyrinthine lies, the character assassinations, the incriminations by assertion could be endlessly repeated with impunity. But this created various brazen ironies. For instance, the Sandinistas accused us of being *vende patria*, people who sell their country to foreigners. But realistically, who was more *vende patria* than the comandantes, thinking and feeling not as Nicaraguans but as a "vanguard" for an expansionist ideology? Who was more *vende patria* than the Sandinistas themselves, allowing Cubans, Bulgarians, East Germans, and the other proxy puppets of the Soviet empire to undertake a massive, systematic invasion of Nicaragua? And what Nicaraguan didn't dream of our national heroes arising furiously from their indignant graves and riding with their ghostly armies to expel these proxy invaders forever?

Orwell in Nicaragua: Elections, Harassment, and Representative Censorship

> "The revolution tolerates ideological pluralism, so long as it doesn't jeopardize its political power. In other words, ideological expressions and their vehicles must disappear in this country by inanition or natural death; we aren't going to decree their extinction.
>
> "But pluralism and a mixed economy are a concession, an act of generosity that is at the same time a political necessity.
>
> "Everyone knows that conceptions of freedom depend on ideological conceptions, and we will never convince the editors at *La Prensa* that, here, they are the main enemies of freedom of the press."
>
> (Tomás Borge, *"La Necesidad de un Nuevo Modelo de Comunicación en Nicaragua"* [The Need for a New Communication Model in Nicaragua]. Closing speech at the *Seminario sobre Comunicación Participativa en la Radio* [Seminar on Participative Communication in the Radio], Managua, 24 November 1984. Published in *Revista de la Escuela de Periodismo*, vol. 1, no. 5 [December 1984: pp. 75-76].)

IN FEBRUARY 1984, we began keeping a statistical record of the percentage of censored material as well as the time it cost us to make revisions. The percentages related to the important first, fifth, and last pages of *La Prensa*. They did not include the sports page, international news (having no relation to Nicaragua), or daily cultural notes. Thus in our percentages, we did not count many things that were censored daily. According to our statistics, censorship was as low as 6.75 percent after the Sandinistas partially lifted the state of emergency for the 1984 elections (19-30 July) and as high as 80 percent during the fifteen days after they announced another state of emergency on 15 October 1985.

The average percentage of censorship was 36.98 for the twenty-seven months *La Prensa* kept statistics: almost thirty-seven of every one hundred pages were censored. In 1986 censorship reached 50 percent. When there were visits to Nicaragua by important visitors such as Jimmy Carter, Carlos Andrés Pérez (former Venezuelan president and member of the Socialist International), or official delegations, censorship was suddenly lowered. But this was for political purposes and hence was the exception rather than the rule. As soon as the people and delegations left, Sandinista censorship resumed.

The censorship figures for 1984 were as follows: February, 23.09 percent; March, 19.30 percent; April, 27.95 percent; May, 30.57 percent; June, 25.77 percent; July, (before the 19th) 45.26 percent, (after the 19th) 6.75 percent; August, 18.80 percent; September, 11.56 percent; October, 15.85 percent; November, 29.37 percent.

We were also unable to publish on the following dates due to excessive censorship:

27 January: Among the news censored were statements made by Arturo Cruz and the Bishops' communiqué about the Christian Brothers' case. (In January 1984, the Ministry of Education refused to allow the Catholic La Salle High School to rehire seven teachers who had been fired by a former director of the school, the pro-Sandinista Christian Brother Edwin Maradiaga.)

1 February: Among the news censored was the case of Bernardino Larios and the revocation of the order that suspended elections. (Former National Guard colonel initially named by the Sandinistas as defense minister and subsequently arrested on trumped-up charges.)

22 March: The central news pertained to an editorial in defense of "the free man." (Orlando Ney Dávila, a Nicaraguan peasant who was televised by the Sandinistas saying, "I am a free man, as free as the light of day." The Sandinistas ran this every evening on their news program. But Dávila was understandably upset, as he had been tricked into providing what seemed to be an endorsement of the Sandinista regime.)

5 April: The primary news dealt with the arrival of Alfredo César in Nicaragua (former president of the Nicaraguan Central Bank, now in exile and a member of the opposition).

18 May: Among items censored was an editorial supporting Luis Mora Sánchez, the *La Prensa* correspondent arrested various times by the government.

31 May: The principal news dealt with the attempted murder of Edén Pastora in Costa Rica.

15 June: We were not allowed to print photographs of floods caused by heavy rains.

18 June: We planned to publish photographs and information about

OPEN (now Sandino City) and the bishops in El Sauce, Nicaragua, for the culmination of the holy year.

10 July: We could not carry primary news about the government's expulsion of ten foreign priests from Nicaragua.

11 July: We prepared primary news about the Pope's condemnation of the expulsions and the disappearance of Father Leplant. (We soon found out he was one of the ten priests expelled by the government.)

After 19 July, the government lifted sections of the state of emergency, and prior censorship was modified for the 1984 elections, which had attracted world attention. But we still could not publish on two dates due to excessive censorship:

6 August: Our main news dealt with *turba* attacks on presidential candidate Arturo Cruz and his supporters in Matagalpa and Chinandega.

22 October: We prepared principal news about the Independent Liberal Party's decision to withdraw from the elections.

The election of 1984 was a Somoza-style election completely controlled and orchestrated by the FSLN. One of the Sandinistas' many tricks was to create a "cushion" of 400,000 nonexistent "ghost" voters. As the Sandinistas controlled all the information, from voter registration to the counting of the ballots, they released a series of contradictory reports that were finally refined into one report of fanciful, cooked figures.

In addition, although the Sandinistas maintained a legal fiction that censorship had been lifted (except for matters of national security), the Nicaraguan Bar Association, an independent group of Nicaraguan attorneys, issued a subsequent report that found the following:

> In the month of July 1984, the approaching electoral period and the ensuing political considerations created a climate of apparent freedom in which the electoral political activity could be carried out in a relatively normal fashion. Thus Decree #1477 was issued *(Gaceta* no. 145, July 26, 1984), reinstating the rights in Art. #15 (freedom of movement), as was Art. #28 (right to hold meetings and demonstrations) and Art. #21 (freedom of speech, but only for the political parties participating in the election). A complementary decree, no. 1480 *(Gaceta* no. 151, August 8, 1984) also reinstated Art. #32 (the right to strike) and Art. #50 (the right of habeas corpus). But citizens did not regain the right either to sue those people or to have adjudicated the laws responsible for the violations of rights

and guarantees committed in the past, which then remained unpunished and unchanged.

It was precisely the aforementioned decrees that gave *La Prensa* the legal basis for seeking the protection of the Supreme Court to free itself from the restrictive prior censorship to which it continued to be subjected, despite the reestablishment of freedom of information (except on military questions that always remained forbidden). Despite the abundant evidence presented...and in express violation of the law that orders the court to grant or deny protection within 45 days, the Supreme Court Justice never passed sentence.

On 29 August 1984 the entire *La Prensa* edition destined for the Western part of the country, comprising the districts of León and Chinandega in an area with large circulation including the port of Corinto, was confiscated by the Sandinista Security forces. They gave no explanation or justification for this action. The edition had been previously approved by the censor. It contained a photostat reproduction of a page from a December 1956 issue of *Poliedro*, edited by Sergio Ramírez (Government Junta member and vice-presidential candidate at the time of the confiscation). The page had an editorial glorifying and eulogizing Anastasio Somoza García, signed by a very close family member of the vice-presidential candidate.

In summary, we can make the following generalizations about the electoral period:

On 19 July 1984, freedom of speech was partially reestablished, with the consequent restriction that "only news related to military matters affecting the security of the nation would require prior authorization by the competent authorities" (Article #2, Part 2, Decree #1477).

This decree was partially obeyed by the censor with the exception of a number of news items on the campaign of the Democratic Coordinating Board's candidate-nominee, Dr. Arturo Cruz, and the announcement of the Independent Liberal Party (PLI)'s withdrawal from the race, and other news on economic matters and human rights violations. Despite these excesses, it may be said that from 19 July to 8 November 1984, censorship was less harsh and arbitrary than in the previous two and one-half years.

But four days after the 4 November elections, the directors of *La Prensa* (together with the other directors of the communications media) were summoned to a private meeting with Communications Media Director Lt. Nelba Blandón—to "orient" us on the new prohibitions in force from that day on.

The guidelines were as follows:

1. Absolute prohibition to refer to the 4 November elections in terms that directly or indirectly express or suggest citizens' abstentions, fraud, manipulation of figures, or lack of confidence in the electoral authorities. Anything referring to the elections must meet the Media Office's criteria.

2. Absolute prohibition of all news and comments on military matters outside of those released by the Ministry of Defense, by the Ministry of the Interior, or by the Government Junta.

3. Absolute prohibition of all news of foreign character, by individuals, prominent persons, foreign governments or organizations, especially and above all the United States, that contain attacks or unfavorable comments tending to weaken the Nicaraguan government, the Sandinista Party, or the Sandinista Popular Revolution.

4. Absolute prohibition of news headlines that do not exactly coincide with the body of the article (although the Media Office always "revised" headlines precisely in this manner).

5. Absolute prohibition of all items on labor problems or strikes.

6. Obligation to publish the dispatches of the Ministry of Defense, the Interior, and the Government Junta.

Moreover, we were told that the above prohibitions had to be obeyed but couldn't be published. Since these were illegal and arbitrary measures, on 14 November 1984 the editorial board of *La Prensa* decided to appeal to the Ministry of Interior, the Media Office's superior authority.

Thirty days passed without an answer to the appeal, so on 19 December 1984 *La Prensa* sought the protection of the Supreme Court in the same terms, asking as well for an injunction until the issue was settled. The Supreme Court accepted the appeal. But it never ruled on the issue, and it refused to order the injunction.

The Protection Law (Decree #417) allows the Supreme Court forty-five days for a ruling. When we started gathering material for this book, the Court was already 450 days overdue. Indeed, the Sandinistas have repeatedly broken their own laws.

In November 1984, the government prevented twenty-four Nicaraguan citizens from leaving the country. All of them were opponents of the regime who either had speaking engagements or other business outside the country. Among the *La Prensa* personnel detained were Carlos Holmann, executive vice-president; Roberto Cardenal, assistant to the editor and secretary of the editorial staff; Pedro Joaquín Chamorro Barrios, acting editor of *La Prensa*, and myself.

Pedro Joaquín's case was typical. As he was about to board a plane at the Managua Sandino Airport on his way to Tokyo, where he was to speak to the World Congress of Journalists, the airport immigration officer stopped him from leaving, "on superior orders," and confiscated his passport.

Pedro Joaquín immediately called the Japanese Embassy, for they had invited him, and he also dialed Comandante Tomás Borge's private, unlisted number, that he still had from less stormy times. Borge was not in. Alarmed, the Japanese Embassy sent its first secretary to the Immigration Office, where he was told that perhaps there was something wrong with the passport and that they would investigate.

Hours later, Pedro's phone rang. Borge wished to know why Pedro had called; Pedro explained. After a few hours, Borge called again and said that the multiple visa on the passport was no longer valid but that he had ordered a new single visa for Pedro so that he could travel the next day.

Around the same date, Dr. Roberto Cardenal, assistant to the editor and secretary of the editorial staff of *La Prensa*, was invited to give a conference on the situation of the church in Nicaragua. At the Sandino Airport, the immigration officer took his passport and began to check it. The cubicles where they check passports are a faithful copy of those at the Moscow airport, and the counter where one hands in the document is neck high: the officer checks it on a table lower than his waist, and thus the traveler cannot see what he is doing. After checking and looking, the officer, very courteous, said: "Mister Cardenal, your passport is torn, and therefore you cannot travel. I am very sorry, but in the passport itself, on the last page, it says among other things, as you can see," showing him the page, "'that any mutilation or alteration immediately makes it void.' You should go at once and request a new passport." Of course, the conference had to be cancelled. Incidents like the above happened various times.

On 15 December, Pedro Joaquín Chamorro Barrios, acting editor of *La Prensa*, went into exile in Costa Rica. Pedro was completely exhausted from the teeming tensions and threats directed against himself and *La Prensa*. He thought that he could be more effective in exile, bringing *La Prensa*'s plight to world attention. In Costa Rica, Pedro addressed an open letter to the comandantes, asking them how they could pretend to tolerate democracy when they would not tolerate one censored newspaper. He criticized the Sandinista mind-set that considered a news item about a ninety-six-year-old woman who committed suicide as an assault against the "psychic health of the people" and hence an assault against "national security." On 15 October 1985 the government confiscated Pedro's house in Managua. After Pedro went into exile, I was named managing editor of *La Prensa*.

A variegated example of Sandinista censorship may be seen in the following examples of news censored in 1984. The headlines are the original ones:

And then they complain of "embargoes"

After the Government House invited *La Prensa* to a ceremony commemorating our Martyred-Editor Pedro Joaquín Chamorro C., the security agents prevented our reporters access to the event. (11 January)

Drug stores have no drugs to sell

The censor suppressed statements from drug store owners, explaining to the public the reason for the lack of medications, such as IV fluids, drugs for the heart and high blood pressure, etc. (11 January)

A new plaza built near the lake

The censor suppressed statements by official spokesperson Ileana Machado, announcing the building of a new plaza on the Xolotlán Lake Shore, at an undetermined cost. (9 February)

Young man dies for not hearing a command to stop

The censor silenced the murder of Salvador Rivas Salazar, shot by a Sandinista traffic cop after giving him the "ominous halt." (23 April)

The "René Cisneros" residents say:
If they could pay for the sign, they can afford the bridge

The censor suppressed the photo of a sign that cost the Managua Reconstruction Board—i.e., the taxpayers, 400,000 *córdobas*. (25 April)

Sandinista Television System asks Jaime Chamorro
Cardenal for an interview, Chamorro Cardenal answers

My letter to the Sandinista Television System, refusing an invitation to participate in a television interview: "After witnessing the slanderous and vulgar campaign launched by the Sandinista Television System...that has left us in utter defenselessness, I am completely convinced that I cannot run the risk of placing myself in your hands. To appear on TV at this time would discredit me with the Nicaraguan people." (7 May)

The fowl and the milk are rotten

Due to the continuous blackouts, the few fowl and scarce milk bags that happen to make it to the county of Catarina are rotten. (12 May)

Confiscations worry the private sector

A UPI dispatch from Managua in which Ramiro Gurdián, president of the Nicaraguan Farmers Association and vice-president of the Superior Council of Private Enterprise (COSEP), asserts that "private enterprise in Nicaragua is a myth"; people are having "their property confiscated simply for being in disagreement with the revolutionary process." (29 May)

Confiscations Worry the Private Sector
Businessmen want "clear talk"

The Federation of the Nicaraguan Chamber of Commerce wishes "to know what is the future of commercial activities in the country"; on the same day, a mother at *La Libertad*, Chontales, asks the government to return to her the only son she has left: she had already lost the other two, Carlos Alberto and Sebastián Soza Arrollo, in combat. (12 June)

Coordinating Board will not enter candidates

Prior to the elections, the censor suppressed a *France Presse* dispatch on the Democratic Coordinating Board's announcement that it would not enter candidates "until the Sandinista government guarantees conditions for a clean and democratic electoral process." (15 June)

Ideas for All

The censor suppressed a section paid for by COSEP, "Ideas for All," comparing the 1974 and 1984 Nicaraguan electoral laws with the current Venezuelan electoral law. (23 June)

Contadora draft foresees "national reconciliation"

The same thing happened to the *Contadora* Draft that mentioned "National Reconciliation" (3 July) and a letter from COSEP to Comandante Tomás Borge, informing him that "as an organization, COSEP is above all interested in good government for the Nicaraguan people, and in particular will protect and strengthen the private sector that yet remains in the country, and towards that end it has the obligation of trying to influence good governmental management, no matter who may be in power." (4 July)

30 JRM workers repair the FSLN sign

An interview with the thirty Managua Reconstruction Board (JRM) workers who, with taxpayers' money, repair the private FSLN (Sandinista Party) sign on the Motastepe Hill, at a cost of several million *córdobas* in galvanized iron, wood, cement, iron rods, wires, and paint—all of which are scarce throughout the country and controlled by the government. (11 July)

Editorial

Our editorial commending an *El País* [Madrid newspaper] editorial that said: "The only real solution for Nicaragua is to allow a period of general freedoms, no matter what the risk may be." (8 August)

Armed Cuban tried to prevent journalist's work

A protest against an "armed Cuban" who, in Las Colinas, prevented journalist Marvin Sequeira from taking a picture of a bus overloaded with passengers. (18 September)

20 UPANIC jeeps in hands of the EPS

The disappearance at the Customs House of twenty diesel jeeps donated by the U.S. government to the private sector for development programs, which the customs officers had turned over to the Sandinista Army. (19 November)

Rionsito: An April Fool's Decree

On April Fool's Day, which Nicaraguans celebrate on 28 December, an innocent *Rionsito* cartoon decrees that "today we are free, sovereign and independent...wouldn't you like it? April Fool!" (28 December) [A rough translation of "the day of the innocents"—the day on which jokes are played, when if someone falls for a joke the response is, "I caught you being innocent," i.e. naïve.]

Because of *La Prensa*, there is no freedom of the press, Chuno Blandón says

A response by the Social Christian Party to the government minion, Chuno Blandón who, on radio and TV programs financed by the government, *El Tren de las Seis* ["The Six O'Clock Train"] and *Línea Directa* ["Direct Line"], continually proclaimed that "Because of *La Prensa's* criticisms, there is no freedom of the press." (Blandón had been director at *Radio Sandino*, the official radio station of the FSLN, since 1979. In 1985, he was relieved of his position when his Somocista past was suddenly remembered.)

As 1984 ended, *La Prensa* had been unable to circulate twelve days, and Sandinista mobs had closed another twenty *La Prensa* distribution points. In the month of December alone, 150 news items had been censored for endangering "the national honor of the Sandinista revolution." Our files of censored materials were so voluminous that even if we had had a full year, *La Prensa* could not have published all the material that had been censored during the previous three years.

Out of the thousands of news items censored by the government in 1984, one was especially memorable: the Sandinistas had selected eleven young Nicaraguans to carry a torch commemorating the anniversary of Nicaragua's independence (15 September). It was a highly publicized celebration, and the Sandinistas had pulled out all the stops to orchestrate the dramatic moment when the Nicaraguan youths would hand over the torch of freedom to Costa Rican authorities gathered on their country's border. As assorted guests and dignitaries from both countries looked on, the eleven people handed the torch to the Costa Rican authorities and then asked for asylum.

Revolutionary Tourism, Spies, and Tapped Telephones

DURING THIS TIME, international support for the Sandinistas was flowing not only from countries behind the iron curtain but from many citizens of the free world. Some of these were undoubtedly motivated by fine sentiments and wanted to right many of the errors and injustices that also exist in the West. But they failed to see the systematic oppression and injustice that the Sandinista government perpetuates—a government that cannot function politically, socially, or economically. The pronouncements of these visitors were, at best, naïve and not closely in touch with Nicaraguan reality.

Governments throughout the Americas and Europe, not wanting to cede influence to the left by default and attempting to either placate or undercut the left in their own countries, also assisted and supported the Sandinistas. The Sandinistas, of course, understood this and were skillful in adapting themselves to each political situation and the circumstances that attended it. They are proficient when it comes to propagating lies and half-truths, manipulating the good will and faith of many people.

The principal function of the Nicaraguan Institute of Tourism is to promote trips to Nicaragua for North Americans and Europeans who want to "understand" the revolution. Thus teachers, professionals, students, workers, ministers, priests, and nuns arrive in Nicaragua in groups of twenty to thirty to penetrate the country's reality in a period ranging from a couple of days to a couple of months.

In all of the programs meticulously arranged for visitors and tourists, a trip to *La Prensa* was considered indispensable. After all, visitors could personally witness an opposition newspaper publishing in Sandinista Nicaragua. This was how the trip to *La Prensa* was usually promoted and in their typical cynical irony, the Sandinistas used *La Prensa* to legitimize themselves. They emphasized that *La Prensa* was an opposition newspaper to prove that Nicaragua was a free country, just as Somoza had used the existence of *La Prensa* to prove that his government was not dictatorial. Of course, as the visitors were carefully whisked in and out of *La Prensa*, it probably did not occur to many of them that the mere existence of a newspaper proves nothing—the more pertinent point is what it is allowed to publish. If an opposition newspaper is allowed to criticize the government, then certain things can be said on behalf of the government that permits genuine criticism. But it is quite different when a government permits a paper to publish only what it has approved, subjecting it to prior censorship and then using the very fact of its existence to imply that there is freedom of the press.

Each week we received two to four groups of visitors, most of them organized by the Institute of Tourism, but some conducted by organizations such as the Center for Promotion and Development (CEPAD), a nominally religious organization that actively supports the government.

At times, there were those who truly wanted to understand what was happening in Nicaragua and who arrived with open minds. Many other visitors, however, arrived with ideological preconceptions that were reinforced by their hosts. They were convinced in advance that the Sandinistas were the best thing that ever happened to Nicaragua. They swallowed completely all the stories and statistics furnished by the Sandinistas and were openly hostile to the staff of *La Prensa*. Basically, they saw what they wanted to see.

These groups also visited other organizations and political parties. In one meeting when Virgilio Godoy, the president of the Independent Liberal Party (and previously minister of labor for four years in the Sandinista government), told the group that the Sandinista TV show *"de Cara al Pueblo,"* in which ordinary citizens supposedly get to ask questions of Sandinista leaders, was arranged beforehand, a newly arrived North American tourist angrily stood up and shouted, "That's a lie!"

On another occasion, a group investigating human rights violations by the Contras visited me. I told them their efforts were both laudable and necessary; then I asked them if they were also investigating violations of human rights by the Sandinistas. They replied in the negative, informing me that they were only investigating violations of human rights by the Contras. I then told them that instead of a human rights group, they seemed to be a human "left" group.

On still another occasion, a group arrived on the same plane with ten Catholic priests who were being forcibly expelled from Nicaragua on that same day. In the meeting held in the offices of *La Prensa*, they asked me my opinion of Reagan's policy toward Nicaragua. I answered that it would have been a pertinent question if Nicaragua were a free country like their own, but that perhaps they wanted to see me in the same position as the ten priests they had seen expelled that morning. Indeed, I had to learn from experience that many of these groups or individuals asked questions solely to obtain compromising statements that could then be used against us. The same statements made in Chile would have been celebrated but ours were often used either to make tendentious ideological points outside the country or as ammunition for the Sandinistas inside the country.

Sometimes these visitors simply invented conversations that never took place. In August 1986 a letter was published in the *New York Times* from a North American who claimed he had just returned from Nicaragua where he had conducted long interviews with Horacio Ruiz, one of *La Prensa*'s top editors. According to the American, Ruiz had said that *La Prensa* supported the overthrow of the Sandinista government and had received money through an organization that was a conduit for the CIA and that *La Prensa* also viewed Contra attacks on unarmed citizens as a legitimate tactic of warfare. Needless to say, Ruiz never made such statements—statements that, besides being untrue, would have immediately landed him in jail.

Whenever I talked to foreigners, I tried to make it clear (if it was not an interview) that we would engage in a frank and honest exchange of opinions that were not for publication. I did not, of course, say anything that would give the government a pretext to imprison me, although I was as candid as I could be under the circumstances. After one of these meetings, the North Americans that had attended it returned to New York and, according to large headlines that subsequently appeared in *Barricada* and *El Nuevo Diario,* published statements they attributed to me.

A few days later I was ordered by Sandinista Security to appear the next day in an office in the Ministry of Interior. When I arrived, I was ushered to an elegant salon and told to wait. As Sandinista soldiers began installing TV cameras, lights, and microphones, I was sure that I would be interrogated and filmed. I was conscious that if I denied what the newspapers had said, the Sandinistas would use my statements for propaganda purposes, but if I confirmed the newspaper accounts, this would constitute for the Sandinistas irrefutable proof of my "counterrevolutionary attitude."

As I pondered this dilemma, I calmed myself by praying mentally. Shortly afterwards, Lenín Cerna, head of Sandinista Security, entered the room, greeted me, and then invited me to sit with him on a couch in front of the TV cameras. After sitting down, I took out a cigar and lit it while he began the interrogation.

"What can you tell me about the reports published in *El Nuevo Diario* and *Barricada* concerning statements you made that were published in New York?"

I took a drag from the cigar and then answered calmly, "Actually, I receive three or four groups of foreigners weekly, but I don't keep a record of everything I say and I don't remember what I said to that particular group but if you want to know what I think I'll be happy to tell you."

Cerna did not reply, so I continued. "I believe that Central America, like other areas in the world, is subjected to a conflict that transcends its borders. Hence citizens of good will are fighting for one cause or another. In El Salvador, for example, there are Salvadorans fighting for communism, and they are assisted by countries promoting this ideology. You yourselves, the Sandinistas, received assistance from Cuba and other countries for your struggle against Somoza. Everyone who believes in a cause has the right to fight for it and to request assistance to achieve it. We won't discuss which system is better, but I do believe that regardless of ideology, people should not be denied the right to choose and to struggle for whatever they believe is best for their country."

As I continued to answer Cerna's questions, I replied without compromising myself. During the "interview," I noted that Cerna was indecisive and vacillating in his questions and, of course, the interview never appeared on Sandinista TV.

At other times, the government tried to turn our employees into spies. One morning I was in my office when a person who worked in the art department entered alarmed and upset. We had absolute confidence in him. He told me that Sandinista Security had approached him, first with blandishments and later with threats, in order to persuade him to become a spy for the Sandinistas inside *La Prensa*.

The Sandinistas didn't want him to compromise private documents or to take papers from our offices; they wanted him simply to inform them about whatever he saw or heard, to note what was said in his particular department, the printing room, or wherever he had access to this type of information. He would be "the eyes and ears" of Sandinista Security at *La Prensa*. Fortunately, he resisted their persuasive pressure.

Other employees were approached in the same manner, and we know of four that resisted the Sandinistas' blandishments and threats but, with one exception, we never knew if the Sandinistas had succeeded in turning some employees into informants.

One afternoon an in-law of mine was having drinks with an agent for Sandinista Security. In a moment of weakness, the agent revealed the identity of an informant inside *La Prensa*: the office boy of Pedro Joaquín Chamorro Barrios, coeditor of *La Prensa*. The office boy was a person we trusted absolutely and who worked within the very heart of *La Prensa*. Through his hands passed all the documents, articles, and letters that were transmitted to Pedro Joaquín.

Our problem was how to determine whether what was said over drinks was true. There was always the possibility that this was a Sandinista scam to discredit a trusted and esteemed employee. Thus we alerted all of the editors and staff members, and began planning a strategy for determining whether or not we were being betrayed. For several days we could not find an appropriate way of testing the office boy, so we "promoted" him to the position of office boy to the financial manager and provided him a higher salary, thus removing him from an office containing sensitive information.

The same day he received his promotion, he resigned indignantly, saying that he refused to be the office boy of an "accountant." Soon after that, we were told he had been employed by the Ministry of Interior, and some of our workers saw him in the streets of Managua wearing the military uniform that employees of the Ministry are required to wear.

In Nicaragua one becomes accustomed to the Sandinistas' ubiquitous spying. One works knowing that the very walls have ears, that the telephones are tapped, and that the mail is opened. This atmosphere creates a fear that even "pillow talk" will end up in the archives of State Security. Many times mail never arrives and when it does it is two or three months late and bears a government seal indicating that it had been received either "open, torn or sealed with adhesive tape."

This transparent government trick occasionally backfires. On 7 November 1981 we published a copy of a mailed envelope sent to Fabio Gadea, at that time president of the Committee for Democracy. The letter had been stamped "received sealed with adhesive tape," but the stamp bearing this slogan appeared *underneath* the tape, clearly indicating that the letter had been opened. We ended our account with the admonition, "Be more careful censor!" On 14 November we published a photo of letters that had been already been opened when they were received by the Social Christian Party. The letters had been sent from different parts of the country, as well as from different countries around the world.

Because the Nicaraguan people know that the mail is systematically violated by the government, they have no confidence in the Sandinista postal service. Consequently, when those who have relatives outside the country learn that a friend or acquaintance is able to travel abroad, they give them letters to be mailed outside Nicaragua. In this way, we are usually able to guarantee the privacy of mail intended for loved ones rather than the Sandinista government. At other times, we are not so fortunate.

At the end of 1983, I traveled to Costa Rica with my wife. In the town of Sapoá, five kilometers from the Costa Rican border, there was a temporary migration post replacing the border post in Peñas Blancas that had been destroyed by rebel forces. As there were no facilities for those who wait while all their belongings are checked by Sandinista Migration, we waited three hours under a large tree while the Migration official read, among other things, all the letters that my wife had been given by friends who had children or relatives in San José, Costa Rica.

It would take too long to relate everything that happened, and it is difficult to describe how the official meticulously scrutinized the notes my wife had made in her Bible or how he insisted that she give him the address of a girl who had written a postcard praising *La Prensa*'s struggle for democracy, urging us not to give up—a postcard that my wife used as a bookmark in the aforementioned Bible.

This postcard was too much for the Migration official who quickly called his superior and told him what he had found. After the latter had returned the postcard to me, I asked him why they read letters and checked books and personal documents. "Look," he told me, "to send letters one has to use the proper channel—the postal service in Nicaragua. Consequently, if a person carries letters by hand, we have to check and read them because it is prohibited to send letters in this way."

The telephone service is also monitored by the government. In *La Prensa* we felt as if we personally knew the Cuban who recorded our phone calls. On one occasion, we tried to make a long-distance call through the operator. Once we had been connected with the other party, the operator said, "One moment please, don't talk yet." As she kept insisting that we shouldn't talk, we finally asked her, "What's wrong? Is the Cuban's tape recorder broken?" On another occasion, our conversation was interrupted by an apparent lack of technical expertise: we heard a screeching noise and then we heard what we had just said played back by a recorder.

In fact, the Sandinistas and their spies never took great care in hiding these violations of privacy, especially after what they did in practice was triumphantly legalized in the decree suspending the *Rights and Guarantees of the Nicaraguan People* on 16 October 1985. Daniel Ortega, president of Nicaragua, personally announced the suspension on Sandinista television.

Before the government mandated prior censorship in 1982, one of our reporters telephoned just before closing time from a labor union office. He spoke with Pedro Joaquín and told him that he had a communiqué that the union had just released which he would bring immediately to *La Prensa*. He requested that space be reserved on the front page and in order to convince Pedro, he read part of the communiqué. Shortly afterwards, Pedro received a call from Tomás Borge, minister of the interior, warning him not to publish the communiqué.

In 1986, *La Prensa* formally applied for permission to transmit on *Radio Corporación* "*La Prensa* on Air," a news program that had been very popular in the times of Somoza. It consisted of a brief summary of the day's principal news for *campesinos* who did not have access to our newspaper. We carefully prepared and filled out all the appropriate forms, making sure we had fulfilled all the legal requirements. As the news items we intended to broadcast came from items in *La Prensa* that had already been submitted to prior censorship and approved, we did not anticipate any objection by the government. Indeed, the government had no objection, but neither did it respond to our application. This is a tactic used frequently by the Sandinistas, even though Sandinista law requires the government and its institutions to reply within a specific time. By ignoring requests or protests, nothing changes or happens.

After we sent various letters that were also ignored, I had a meeting with the director of the Media Office, Nelba Blandón, and asked for a reply to our application. With a sarcastic smile, Blandón replied, "You're dreaming if you think I'm going to respond to the request." I then asked her what objections she had, and she answered, "There are sufficient objections in *La Prensa*; why do you need more?"

Indeed, Blandón enjoyed joking about matters that we frequently had to discuss or arrange with her. But one day, she became enraged after I pretended to make a joke, suggesting that she ask her Cuban advisers to take less time censoring *La Prensa*. After she had disdainfully responded that the Media Office had no Cuban advisers, I paused deliberately and then replied, "Well, excuse me, but since I see Cuban advisers in the army, in all the Ministries, in the public offices, and even the Supreme Court—I thought that the Media Office would not be the exception."

Blandón smiled broadly and said, "In the army and the Ministries, the Cubans supply the technical expertise that we lack, but if in Cuba there are no [independent] newspapers, what can the Cubans teach us about journalism?"

"Well," I said, "they seem to be teaching you to achieve the same results."

We tried not to lose our sense of humor, but it was inevitable that the government would censor even that, as they did when they began censoring a popular comic strip called *Rionsito*, which poked fun at Sandinista hypocrisy. By the beginning of 1985, it seemed that even laughter was being strangled in a country that was slowly suffocating. For *La Prensa*, it was the beginning of the end.

The Beginning of the End

ON 2 JANUARY 1985 the government inaugurated the new year by censoring 80 percent of all our submitted copy. Among the censored items was an announcement from the Ministry of Interior that all international airplane tickets would have to be purchased in dollars—the government was again censoring itself. We were unable to publish because of excessive censorship on 8 and 9 January. Consequently, our 230 employees stopped work on 10 January to protest publicly the government censorship that had prevented circulation for two days in that week. In a letter sent to president Daniel Ortega, the workers asked him to permit all of *La Prensa's* employees to work freely—without pressures, threats, or restrictions. On 8 and 10 April, excessive censorship again prevented *La Prensa* from circulating. Likewise on 6 May, 80 percent of our copy was censored, particularly news about Daniel Ortega's trip to the Soviet Union. On 5 June *La Prensa* protested both the illegal confiscation of *Saimsa*, a corporation run by the Bolaños family that provided agricultural services, and another government plot to discredit *La Prensa*. We could not publish. On 10 June, we officially requested that prior censorship be lifted.

Because no censored materials can appear in the Nicaraguan media, we used to distribute the censored materials to foreign journalists, embassies, independent unions, and friends. A total of 150 copies were sent by messenger two or three times a week. But on 27 November 1985, Captain Nelba Blandón sent a threatening letter ordering us to cease distributing these materials, especially to foreign journalists and embassies. Blandón threatened us with thirty-year prison sentences if we continued endangering "the security of the nation." She accused us of, among other things, distributing cables written by foreign journalists and carried by major news services such as Associated Press and United Press International. Blandón even brazenly pretended that these cables had not appeared outside the country.

On 2 December, in protest against the rigid censorship and the government's incessant threats, *La Prensa* didn't circulate. The Sandinistas arbitrarily closed *La Prensa* on 7 December for two days, without specifying the alleged decree or law that had supposedly been violated. They sometimes did this for intimidation—to show us they could close *La Prensa* whenever they wanted. By 10 December, the government had begun dictating the letter-type *La Prensa* was to use in publishing. In all, *La Prensa* could not be published ten times due to forced closings, excessive censorship, or protests of our own against censorship.

In six years, the Sandinistas had closed *La Prensa* ten times, exceeding the combined record of the Somoza dynasty, which had either closed or censored *La Prensa* nine times (for varying periods) during the forty-three years of its dictatorial reign.

Censorship figures for 1985 were as follows: January, 44.32 percent; February, 49.93 percent; March, 28.32 percent; April, 23.01 percent; May, 60.85 percent; June, 44.14 percent; July, 35.71 percent; August, 37.03 percent; September, 43.27 percent; October, 80 percent; November, 55.90 percent; December, 50 percent.

The Sandinistas often manipulated technology so that their victims could be made to appear in compromising situations or to be making compromising statements. For instance, I was interrogated on 23 March by Lenín Cerna, head of Sandinista State Security, and videotaped. The government had videotaped other *La Prensa* personnel before. After the video taping, Cerna made a melodramatic press statement in which he ordered "strict vigilance" of me for my supposed links with rebel groups. This was absurd. I had no links with rebel groups, and Cerna and the Sandinistas knew it. But the Contra label was one of their favorites, ranking almost with the supremely popular "agent of the CIA."

In March 1985, *La Prensa* was awarded a one-year grant of $100,000 from the National Endowment for Democracy (NED). In 1986, before we were closed, we received $50,000, the first half of a second grant for $100,000. The Sandinista government had refused to sell us the foreign currency necessary for the importation of raw materials. It had closed down or threatened many of our distribution points, restricted our paper supply, and refused to transfer our money to our supplier in New

York. Thus we were grateful for a grant for which the Sandinista government had ironically created the conditions. We did not receive any of the money directly. Instead, it went to our supplier who, in turn, shipped us the ink, chemicals, and other raw materials necessary for publishing a newspaper. The grants were publicly announced by the donor. Nevertheless, the Sandinistas used the ensuing publicity to assert that *La Prensa* was receiving money from CIA agencies and continued to repeat this transparent lie as an "established fact." Because the Sandinistas and their supporters have created multitudinous myths, I would like to respond to this one in detail.

First, the NED is a private nonprofit grant making organization which has received an annual appropriation from the U.S. Congress since 1984 and has a bipartisan board of directors that includes Dante B. Fascell, Lane Kirkland, and Walter Mondale. One of its purposes is to assist democracy in countries that have dictatorial governments, such as Chile and Paraguay.

Second, these grants were accepted solely because the Sandinistas did not authorize us the foreign currency needed to purchase raw materials.

Third, these grants were given without any strings or conditions attached.

Fourth, if the Sandinistas question a grant given, without conditions, then we also have a right to question why *Barricada* and *El Nuevo Diario* may receive donations of paper and financial assistance from "socialist" countries; to ask why *Barricada* may receive a printing press from the Communist party of East Germany and employ "internationalists," without being accused of foreign penetration or the selling of their country; to question the ideological double standards of a government that receives foreign aid and military assistance from totalitarian governments alien and hostile to the rights, beliefs, and values of the Nicaraguan people.

Finally, all gifts or grants from any international body, whether governmental or private, must be approved in advance by the Sandinista government and the funds must be deposited in the Central Bank of Managua. (We received no funds: The money went directly to our supplier, who shipped us the necessary raw materials.) In fact, the Sandinista government, which controls foreign funds and grants through the Central Bank in Managua (all the banks in Nicaragua are nationalized), approved the NED grant. Thus, according to the Sandinistas' own procrustean logic, the government has implicated itself in a nefarious CIA plot to destabilize itself.

On 15 October 1985 the Sandinista government declared a new state of emergency, officially suspending a series of rights and guarantees that had already been suspended in practice. For instance, we at *La Prensa* had known for a long time that our mail was either opened or destroyed and that our office and home phones were tapped. The right of habeas corpus had existed in name only since 1979. During the month of October, the government censored 80 percent of everything we submitted. Even Daniel Ortega's public announcement that he would meet with President Reagan in New York was censored, although the pro-Sandinista media was allowed to report it. After submitting the day's issue, we had to wait an average of six and a half hours for the censor's decision.

During this time, the Sandinistas had repeatedly insisted that the Contras were on the verge of being annihilated, and their supporters abroad had repeatedly said that the Contras had never held "one inch" of Nicaraguan territory—that they had no chance of winning the war. If this is so, then there was and is no reason or justification for a perpetual state of emergency; there was and is no reason for prior censorship, and there was and is no reason or justification for the closing of *La Prensa* on 26 June 1986. Only a hegemonic government obsessed with monolithic conformity would insist that one restricted newspaper, subjected to prior censorship, threatened national security.

The Nicaraguan Bar Association summarized the state of emergency in these terms:

> On October 16, 1985, President Daniel Ortega, assisted by his minister of justice, Ernesto Castillo, issued on television a new State of Suspension of Rights and Guarantees contained in several articles of the Fundamental Statute of the Republic. Most unusual is the fact that said decree, to date, has not been published in writing, and, therefore, its true text is not known with certainty. [The decree was published once, however, in *Barricada*, 16 October 1985, p. 5.]
>
> It is known that, again, the right to strike, to hold peaceful meetings, the freedom of movement, habeas corpus, and the Supreme Court's protection for the stay of unlawful proceedings, and, of course, free speech and freedom of information are also among those that have been suspended. Moreover, the Vice President, Doctor Ramirez Mercado, in subsequent appearances on TV, trying to palliate or diminish the gravity of the measure when facing a considerable and unexpected national and international reaction, took upon himself the task of interpreting and modifying the decree, which only created more confusion. We must call attention to the government's lack

of legislative seriousness—a government that frequently issues, reforms, or repeals laws by means of a speech at the plaza or on radio and TV, so that citizens have no opportunity to ascertain the true text of the law. *La Gaceta*, the official journal that was created precisely for that, has been reduced to a simple Administrative Ads sheet where laws are also published, long after they are issued.

Fifteen days after the Nicaraguan Bar Association's Report was made public and twenty-three days after the decree they denounced had been issued, it was finally published in *La Gaceta*, Official Journal No. 215, 8 November 1985, as "Decree #128, State of National Emergency," dated and "enacted" on 15 October 1985. This decree suspends the few rights not suspended before. Besides those already mentioned in the Bar of Lawyers' Report, it suspends individual freedom and personal security, civil and judicial rights, the inviolability of the mails and other types of communication that are often a form of freedom of speech—as well as the freedom of movement and the right to freely choose one's place of residence, the inviolability of private life, of the family, and of the home.

Between 1985 and 1986, various *La Prensa* reporters were imprisoned on trumped up charges: Luis Mora Sánchez and photographer Jorge Ortega Rayo, for having allegedly worked for the counterrevolution (Mora had been imprisoned three times before; the first and fourth times, he was savagely beaten, either by Sandinista guards or by prisoners encouraged by the guards); Norman Talavera, for having cooperated in the publication of a censored Catholic newspaper (the Sandinistas were trying to intimidate Talavera so that he would no longer cover church events for *La Prensa*); Máximo Guillermo Alonso for planning to publish a new mimeographed newsletter called *Prisma*; Alejandro Cordonero, Enrique García, and José Ramírez Artola, for publishing *Prisma*. All three were interrogated for fifteen days exclusively about their work at *La Prensa*. (In December 1986, state security police came to the house of García to warn him to stop printing another small, informative bulletin that he produced in his house to earn money. García had no employment once *La Prensa* was closed on 26 June 1986. The security forces threatened him with prison and accused him of being a "Somocista.") We were forbidden to publish a word about any of these arrests.

We were also frequently prevented from publishing rebuttals of Sandinista lies, but the Sandinistas forced us to publish their rebuttals when they were criticized. For instance, on 27 August 1985, *La Prensa* published a letter from a reader commenting on an article that had appeared in the official Sandinista newspaper *Barricada* criticizing the administrative bureaucracy and waste in the recently inaugurated Victoria de Julio sugar cane mill (partially destroyed by fire in January 1988). The vice-minister of MIDINRA [Ministry of Agriculture, Animal Husbandry and Agrarian Reform], in charge of that mill, sent us a letter that was insultingly inappropriate. *La Prensa* answered the vice-minister's letter, explaining to him that our comments applied specifically to the criticism published by *Barricada*, and that that newspaper, not us, should publish his response. We then received a letter from the Media Office, ordering us either to publish MIDINRA's letter or cease publishing that afternoon. Similar incidents happened all the time.

The censorship files in 1985 were even more voluminous than those of previous years. With the total control of the media and, by now, the systematic oppression of all the independent sectors of Nicaraguan society, as well as the coercive attempt to create a society and culture alien and abhorrent to the vast majority of the Nicaraguan people, the Sandinistas implemented what can be characterized as the Stalinization of culture. As their ideological predecessors realized, the Sandinistas understand that language creates our perception of reality. By censoring ideas and news and ensuring that only their language is spoken, written, read, and heard, reality becomes what they say it is. And because Marxism-Leninism is a profoundly expansionist ideology, it is equally obsessed with expressing its own version of reality outside its controlled borders. The propaganda extravaganzas, the lies, and character assassinations are also aimed at manipulating international opinion and silencing critics abroad with bludgeoning words in lieu of the domestic truncheon.

At the beginning of the year, in mid-January 1985, the caption "In the film 1984, convicts confess on TV," was suppressed in *La Prensa*, as was the information that the government was shipping great quantities of food and material out of our impoverished country to Cuba. According to bills of lading at the port of Corinto, during 1984, the following products that are scarce throughout Nicaragua were shipped to Cuba: 5,000 sacks of onions, 43,000 rolls of wire, 12,000 crates of nails, 12,300 boxes of shoes, 1,050 boxes of tobacco leaves, 5,150 boxes of instant coffee, 443 crates of tires and inner tubes, 7,500 barrels of formol, 1,500 boxes of ginger, 123,200 sacks of coffee beans, 63,000 bales of cotton, and assorted undetermined quantities of other products such as toilet tissue, soap, hides, beef, fish, shellfish, woods, furniture, and farm machinery.

The Beginning of the End

In addition, the following representative items were censored in *La Prensa*. They are quoted in full.

CUBANS' NEIGHBORS FRUSTRATED BY "CONSTANT DISTURBANCES"

October 16, 1985

Chinandega—Neighbors of a residence occupied by Cubans cannot find anyone they can appeal to in order to protest the Cubans' constant disturbances.

The residence that belongs to Dr. Domingo Tuckler Martinez, located in the Guadalupe district, is currently being used to house a large number of Cubans.

The neighbors note that, late last Thursday night, the Cubans arrived banging the doors and causing a terrific disturbance.

Furthermore, another house that was owned by Mr. Leonidas Zamora has also been converted into a dwelling for Cuban physicians, who are similarly committing abuses.

At about 11:00 P.M. on Friday night, several of these doctors were driving about on the town's streets in a red Toyota, at high speed, jeopardizing the few passers-by who venture out on the streets at night.

SHORTAGES OF BASIC GOODS REPORTED

October 30, 1986

León—For several days, the absence of plain and sweet bread has been noticed both in bakeries and in grocery stores and among street vendors. According to the León bakers, MICOIN [Ministry of Commerce and Industry] has reduced their monthly quota of flour by 36 percent, forcing the bakeries to operate only three days a week, while maintaining full pay for the workers.

Mr. Sergio Rueda, director of the Ministry of Industry's Food Department in Region 2, admitted the cut that has been made in the flour supply, adding that this situation will continue until November because the arrival of a ship loaded with wheat coming from a Socialist country is expected the following month.

In addition to the flour, there is also a shortage of cooking oil, which they claim is due to the flaws in the AGROSA machinery, from which this region is supplied. The regional head of supplies for MICOIN, Daniel Cáceres, said that this production would return to normal within two weeks.

Insofar as beans are concerned, although it is true that there is a sufficient supply in the shops, the people are not asking for them because they are from Thailand and have a taste different from the native variety.

RAINS DAMAGE CROPS
November 1, 1985

Engineer Rosendo Díaz Bendaña, a member of the board of directors of the Agricultural and Livestock Producers Union of Nicaragua (UPANIC), told *La Prensa:* "At the present time, it is very difficult to make an assessment of the possible damage that this storm has caused to agriculture, primarily because the farm owners have not yet made any report."

"If the rain continues, all the crops will be damaged; for example, the rice would presumably be dragged along by the streams in various farming areas; and in the case of cotton, if it continues raining, the cotton boll would rot."

The rain is also affecting coffee. It is being knocked off the bush while it is still maturing, hence losing quality and value. In any event, the agricultural-livestock producer said, if the rainfall continues, the damage will be sizable, "...but we are unable to estimate it yet, because we have no assessment, and this cannot be known until next week."

The farming areas most affected at present by the storm are Chinandega and León, where there are large plantations of cotton, rice, beans, and other staple grains.

Insofar as the cotton is concerned, another problem seriously threatening the crops is the white fly, which is devastating the plantations; and, in view of the shortage of insecticides, the situation is becoming highly complicated and very dangerous for the cotton producers.

PASSENGERS COMPLAIN OF HIGH TAXI FARES, LACK OF SERVICE
November 2, 1985

Taxi fares have become uncontrollable, because they are not set according to law, asserted customers, who cannot obtain this service unless they pay an extra, prohibitive payment.

A lady complained that the driver of a red taxi with plate 257 told her he would charge her one hundred *córdobas* to take her from the corner of the Colonial Theater to Colonia Centroamérica. When she agreed, he replied that he would not take her despite the fact that his cab was empty, and he took off, but not before having offered her the service for 150 *córdobas*.

The complainant said: "This is blackmail and an abuse that should be punished by law."

Other customers claim that taxi service in the capital has disappeared, and that the Ministry of Transportation has not controlled the rate, which is currently thirty *córdobas* per ride through a zone. But the fact is that drivers are charging a minimum of fifty *córdobas*, and when 7:00 P.M. arrives, most of them do not provide services.

Taxi service at night commands a price of between 1,000 and 1,500 *córdobas*, and more when sick persons seeking assistance in hospitals are involved, as has been confirmed.

SANDINISTA AND INDEPENDENT STUDENT GROUPS CLASH
November 3, 1985

A new feud broke out between the members of the National Union of Students (UNE) and the Sandinista Youth *(Juventud Sandinista-19 de Julio)* at the National Autonomous University of Nicaragua, on 31 October, when the latter virtually ejected the president of UNE, Alberto Cuadra, from the campus. In reprisal, Cuadra refused to turn over the keys to the UNE offices.

The university campus includes the facilities of the School of Humanities, the School of Journalism, the School of Psychology, and the School of Sociology.

As may be recalled, Alberto Cuadra was elected president of UNE this year by a small number of votes, which was not sufficient to allow him to undertake a series of programs that he had offered to put into effect while he was a candidate.

The opposition that Cuadra has encountered has come partly from the defeated members of the Sandinista Youth. This lack of understanding between the two organizations has caused outdoor battles to break out during the past two weeks, especially during nighttime activities.

On Wednesday, 30 October, Cuadra issued a communiqué which was received with great displeasure by the Sandinista Youth; consequently, there was a dispute over the possession of the students' main office.

Cuadra started to leave, but took the keys, which is why the Sandinista Youth removed the locks from the offices and installed chains so as to prevent any further entry by the UNE president.

The university authorities have already been informed of what is going on between UNE and the Sandinista Youth and have undertaken an investigation which they must complete during the month of November. They want to settle the case because they believe that it does not suit either the higher interests of education or Sandinista policy.

SECURITY POLICE INTERROGATE CHURCH, BUSINESS, LABOR LEADERS

November 11, 1985

The arrest of [La Prensa] journalist Norman Talavera Sunday night was one of many arrests and interrogations which State Security has been carrying out for several days.

More than 70 persons have been arrested in an unprecedented action by State Security. Politicians, businessmen, jurists, priests, trade union leaders, and others have been the victims of these actions.

Monsignor Bismarck Carballo was cited, arrested, and interrogated by the chief of Security [Lenín Cerna] after COPROSA, the Church's Social Welfare office, was occupied militarily by State Security.

The politicians arrested included Dr. Luis Rivas Leiva, of the Social Democratic Party, who was warned to stop certain activities and to adhere to the provisions of the the Emergency Law.

Conservative leader Mario Rappaccioli was another of the persons cited and interrogated by Security, in addition to the well-known jurist, Dr. Enrique Meneses Peña, who is president of the Center for Unity and the Promotion of Democracy and Member of the Board of Directors of the Constitutionalist Liberal Party.

Dr. Meneses Peña was arrested and interrogated for three consecutive days, fingerprinted, and then released.

The trade union leaders included members of the Central Organization of Nicaraguan Workers (CTN), who were interrogated in their homes, which were searched.

Alvin Guthrie Rivers, the top leader of the Trade Union Unification Confederation, was cited, interrogated, fingerprinted, and threatened.

The leaders of the independent CGT [General Confederation of Labor] were also searched and interrogated, and Alejandro Solórzano, a member of that organization, is still in prison as the result of a hunger strike for the Nicaraguan workers' Christmas bonus.

Other persons arrested were Francisco Ortega, a well-known merchant from Chinandega, who has already been released, and Prof. Ramón Pichardo, who lectures on human relations.

Rufo Reyes, who had set up a brand new repair shop called "NASA," was also arrested, fingerprinted, interrogated, and expelled from the country, because he is of Peruvian nationality.

Reyes was expelled for composing several songs in honor of Pope John Paul II and Cardinal Miguel Obando y Bravo.

Dr. Marvin Caldera, a well-known industrialist and member of the Charismatic Assemblies and El Carmen Church, was another person arrested, interrogated, and later released.

Finally, Dr. Alberto Saborío, a well-known Managua attorney, was also interrogated and arrested.

VETERINARIANS ASSOCIATION ELECTS OFFICERS
November 12, 1985

On October 28, 1985, an election was held by the Association of Veterinarians to fill two vacancies left by Drs. Humberto Martínez and William Argüello, who were serving as president and secretary, respectively, and who for personal reasons are abroad.

The vacancies left were filled by Drs. José María Cerna Obregón and Rafael Hurtado, completing the association's board of directors, which now is as follows: President, Dr. José María Cerna O.; Vice President, Dr. Arturo Prado; Secretary, Dr. Rafael Hurtado; Treasurer, Dr. Bayardo Fletes; First Director, Dr. Cristóbal Dedemadis; Second Director, Dr. Roy Padget López; Third Director, Dr. Emilio Enríquez.

At its first meeting, this board which is integrated with CONAPRO [National Confederation of Professional Associations] will offer a tribute to five veterinarians who have completed 25 years of professional service.

EVANGELICALS' MEETING DISRUPTED BY MOBS
November 14, 1985

Groups armed with clubs and stones disrupted the meeting where on the night of Tuesday, 12 November, the Evangelical Campaign of the Seven Seals was being held.

The campaign, which is being held 11-18 November, had received the required authorization, according to statements made today by evangelicals who were surprised by such action.

On Tuesday night the police arrived at about 7:00 P.M. and later youths armed with clubs and stones attacked the 300 persons who were at the meeting place, which is situated near Zumen.

Guillermo Sandoval, an evangelical minister and the person responsible for giving talks on the "Great Apocalyptic Campaign and the Divine Holiness," was arrested as the result of this incident; however, he has already been released, according to our sources.

The individuals who disrupted the meeting broke streetlights, cut the electric cables, and were finally arrested by the police.

"We had constructed a platform, a pulpit, and had a collection box in which all of us deposited a sum of money; and approximately 200,000 *córdobas* were lost from it, without any explanation," said one of the evangelicals who was in the Tabernacle of the Seven Seals.

PARENTS PROTEST REQUIRED PURCHASE OF NEWSPAPERS
November 14, 1985

Tipitapa (Belarmino)—Several parents of this town have approached us to report that they cannot tolerate certain school teachers who are requiring their children to buy *Barricada* and *El Nuevo Diario* every day.

"We are too poor to be paying 600 *córdobas* per month for the purchase of those newspapers," one of the complainants stated and then added: "In those newspapers and at the command of the teachers, our children are studying political subjects which favor only the interests of the current rulers."

Another of the complainants said: "We parents have barely enough money to feed our children badly with the little we earn; if the government wishes to continue politicizing our children, then let it assume the costs which up to now we parents have borne for the purchase of those political newspapers."

RESISTANCE AMONG 'VOLUNTEER' COFFEE PICKERS REPORTED
November 24, 1985

There is a great deal of unrest among the state employees who were notified of their "voluntary" mobilization for coffee picking, and who will presumably leave for the northern mountains and the central zone on 26 November.

The harvesting of the "little red beans" is apparently causing serious difficulties for the administrators of the coffee plantations, particularly on the so-called State Production Units (UPE), where the required number of pickers is lacking.

The difficulty is being experienced by the heads of the National Employees Union (UNE) in all the ministries, who cannot find arguments to convince the employees to go to the plantations and pick coffee.

Not even veiled threats made by certain leaders have succeeded in influencing the employees, some of whom claim that, if they are mobilized, they would prefer to resign, because they are skilled workers, specialists, and professionals—not plantation laborers.

The latest compulsory meetings at the state work centers have been marked with absenteeism, because the UNE leadership has been unable to gather enough people to hear shopworn expressions about "aggression, imperialism, and mercenary attacks."

At least the majority of the ministries will be closed temporarily, while others will be closed permanently, or so long as the harvesting of coffee is going on. In other ministries, the closing will take place in certain departments, according to the regional directors of the state union.

A large number of state employees and officials confirmed that they are unwilling to be mobilized for the picking, and those with a family to support and children to care for, in the case of women, are even less willing to do so.

Most of the employees queried on the subject said that they prefer to resign rather than to go to the plantations for the picking. Others, who are undoubtedly leaders of the FSLN party organizations, enthusiastically declare that they are willing to go, "to face the consequences."

Most of the employees and officials appeared extremely annoyed and anxious over the announcement of the closing of the ministries.

PERMISSION REQUIRED TO VISIT EMBASSIES
December 10, 1985

Effective this week, any person who needs to visit any foreign embassy in the country must have authorization from the Central Office for the Protection of Embassies, we have learned.

Members of the Embassy Protection Corps said that with the exception of diplomats and journalists, all persons will have to go to the above-mentioned office, which is located in Las Colinas, and explain the reason for the visit in order to determine whether it merits approval.

For their part, journalists and diplomats will also be required to telephone the Central Office to explain the reason for their visit to avoid major delays.

It is assumed that this new measure has been taken to prevent new cases of [political] asylum like the one which occurred last week at the

Venezuelan Embassy, where several persons took refuge. Among these were one member of the Sandinista army and his family.

The Embassy Protection Corps has been beefed up at all embassies with democratic leanings, especially the embassies of Venezuela, Honduras, Costa Rica, and Guatemala.

Moreover, since last week, young males waiting their turn outside the Honduran Embassy to request a visa to enter that country have been arrested and their passports have been confiscated.

For its part, the Honduran Embassy said officially that reinforcement of police surveillance probably represents reprisals taken for what the government of Nicaragua considers a violation of the dignity of its embassy in Honduras: journalists were permitted to take photos of the building and its personnel, on the day of the recent presidential elections.

The Government of Nicaragua based its protest on Article 22 of the Vienna Convention, which states that the tranquility of personnel at foreign missions should not be disturbed, but the Government of Honduras replied that it does not consider such action to be illegal because there is unrestricted freedom of the press in Honduras.

In addition, the Government of Honduras was able to prove that journalists who took photos were not Hondurans but were from foreign newspapers covering the electoral process in Honduras.

PHARMACISTS IN FINANCIAL STRAITS, GOVERNMENT ACTION REQUESTED

December 13, 1985

The National Association of Pharmacy Owners, reacting to the crisis being experienced by its members, has sent letters requesting an interview with the president of the republic and the minister of health; however, despite the fact that several weeks have elapsed, the association has not received a reply.

The pharmacists wish to inform these authorities about a series of problems that are hampering their daily activities, all of which are performed for the benefit of the people in general.

The pharmacists claim that their receipts are insufficient to pay their bills, including the wages of employees and taxes for the state.

The pharmacists also insist that the "People's Pharmacies," which were established by the Ministry of Health, do not work night shifts [*no hacen turnos*] as the private pharmacies are obliged to do; and that this is an injustice.

HARASSMENT BY MASAYA SECURITY POLICE REPORTED
December 18, 1985

Leonardo Salazar, a native of Tisma, reported that he is being harassed by the Masaya State Security force, which has brought him in for questioning four times so far this year.

"I am going to report the harassment that I have received, as have other Tisma families. We are being accused of participating in incidents which occurred when young men were taken away for military service," he said.

Tisma was one of the towns most opposed to the military service law, and the mothers of that town engaged in heated protests last year.

The last citation Salazar received was December 14, 1985. Among other things, he was asked whether he was a Catholic and whether he believed in the revolution. "I told them that I only believe in God and that I have nothing to do with the revolution."

Salazar said that because of his answers he was threatened by his interrogator; therefore, he fears that he will be arrested again, because following the aforementioned incidents he was detained for one month and charged with being one of the leaders of this movement.

Leonardo Salazar's nephew, Gamali Salazar, has also been detained for four months in the *Zona Franca* on the same charge. Another member of the family whose name is Salazar Arana is also being harassed in that town.

"I have a wife and five children, and it is not just that they have to endure this anxiety. I have asked the authorities to leave me in peace and to allow me to work for my family," he said finally.

MASAYA SECURITY POLICE INTERROGATE MEMBERS OF CATHOLIC CHURCH
December 19, 1985

The principal members of the Catholic congregation of the city of Niquinohomo were notified in writing to report to the State Security offices in Masaya, which are located in the former Social Club of that city.

Notification was made at 7:00 A.M. last Thursday, and the following persons were required to report at 10:00 A.M. the same day: Dr. Rolando Avendaño Sandino; the esteemed lady, Lastenia Zambrana de Valerio; Dámaso Rivas; Augusto César Zambrana; Augusto Muñoz; Prof. Sabas Centeno and his wife; Norman Miranda, president of the Knights of the

Holy Sacrament; and Edwin Alvarado, who could not report because he has had a back operation.

All of them were interrogated about their religious activities and their friendship with the town parish priest. One woman was asked why the priest ate at her home, why she held the position of president of the Holy Sacrament congregation, and who her relatives were.

Since Edwin Alvarado was not able to report for questioning, State Security agents went to his home where he told them he could not get out of bed; nevertheless, they interrogated him right there.

Because Miranda is president of the Knights of the Holy Sacrament, they took front and side view photos of his face and also forced him to be fingerprinted.

The Catholic populace of Niquinohomo is concerned about these unprecedented actions, for they fear imprisonment because of religious beliefs.

HIGH PRICES DRIVE LIQUOR CONSUMPTION DOWN
December 19, 1985

The consumption of liquor has decreased a bit due to price rises last week, *La Prensa* learned from a survey conducted of several Managua liquor stores.

"After the price rise, we saw sales drop a bit. Previously we sold two or three cases a day, but now it is down to one, in spite of the fact that we are in the holiday season," said Mrs. Marta Castañeda, of the Lorena Liquor Store.

The liquor prices authorized by the Directorate General of Revenue were a surprise to no one, as price increases are always announced on holidays.

A bottle of extra dry rum now costs from 500 to 540 *córdobas* in liquor stores and supermarkets, since prices vary from one place to another. The prices of other rums such as Plata and Oro have also been raised.

In another liquor store in Colonia Salvadorita, the proprietor said that even though sales have dropped a little, he expects them to go up again at any time, since this always happens with every price rise.

"First, the people resist buying at higher prices; but afterward they become accustomed to them and start buying again; thus, we hope that our clients will buy their liquor for the Christmas holidays," he said.

We talked with Doña Iris who has one of these stores near the Colonial traffic lights. She too agreed that sales have dropped a little but that they would soon go up as usual.

"Most people do their buying on December 24 and 31; hence, we are expecting a great recovery," another liquor store owner said.

The situation in bars and restaurants appears normal, although the owners of these establishments are pessimistic and are expecting sales to drop in January.

The atmosphere on these holidays is festive, and there is more money in circulation, so the price rises have not caused much concern among the clientele of bars and restaurants, where the prices of liquor are higher.

HUMAN RIGHTS COMMISSION (CPDH) REPORTS INCREASE IN COMPLAINTS

December 20, 1985

During the month of November, the Permanent Commission on Human Rights received various denunciations, which have increased since the state of emergency took effect.

The denunciations reveal that pressure is being principally applied on religious and political sectors that are critical of the Sandinista government.

Forty individual arrests by the Directorate General of State Security were reported to the CPDH, in addition to the arrest of 50 peasants from Nueva Guinea and 40 more peasants from the Estelí region.

The torture and mistreatment of nine common prisoners were also denounced. Cases were also reported of citizens being detained as hostages pending the arrest or voluntary surrender of family members being sought.

In November, more than a dozen Catholic priests were issued summonses by State Security and were warned "that they could not criticize the state of emergency or participate in religious demonstrations without authorization from the Ministry of Interior." These priests were fingerprinted and photographed.

Residents of Chinandega also reported the arrest in November of dozens of persons who were members of the welcoming committee for Cardinal Miguel Obando y Bravo, when he made a pastoral visit to that city on December 10. Eight leaders of this committee were arrested for this reason.

GOVERNMENT EMPLOYEES' PAY WITHHELD
FOR NOT PICKING COFFEE
December 20, 1985

Employees of the Ministry of Housing and Human Settlements (MINVAH) have protested about the measures being taken against those who fail to pick coffee. The latter say that they had been notified a few days ago that they should "voluntarily" go to pick coffee, but they did not expect those who did not respond to be penalized. These penalties, which consist in the docking of their salaries, are being applied against those employees who did not answer the call.

In some other cases brought to our attention, the number of days they fail to pick coffee after being notified will be deducted from their vacation time.

The MINVAH employees say that those who fail to go to pick coffee will have other penalties levied against them, including dismissal.

"Many of us didn't go to pick coffee because we had no one who could watch our children. We can't leave them by themselves, especially since most of us women have small children that need our care," several mothers said.

GOVERNMENT INSPECTOR THREATENS MARKET WORKER
December 21, 1985

A humble worker named Luis Acevedo Morales, who earns his living transporting goods in a cart to the Jinotepe market, told *La Prensa* that he had been threatened with a revolver by MICOIN [Ministry of Commerce and Industry] Inspector Guillermo González Thursday morning, 19 December.

According to Acevedo, he was transporting three loads [*medios*] of wheat to vendor Auxiliadora Tapia when he was threatened by this inspector, who also warned that he would be put in jail if he returned to the town market.

WOMAN LIVING WITH CUBAN SHOT, DETAILS UNCERTAIN
December 26, 1985

Investigations into the case of a young woman who allegedly committed suicide on December 13, 1985, in Rivas have not uncovered a thing, according to information supplied by Flora Enríquez, mother of the victim.

According to Mrs. Enríquez, her daughter, Leonora Enríquez, 23, apparently committed suicide after having had a discussion with a Cuban with whom she had been living for a year. "I suspect that she didn't commit suicide, because neither the watchman nor the other Cuban who were at the Nagualpa farm in Rivas, where they spent the last night, heard a shot."

The young woman had worked as a secretary on a PROAGRO farm where the Cuban also works. He is a veterinarian named Francisco Valdés. The day of the incident, according to our source, many persons said they had seen them in San Jorge talking. Afterward they went to the farm where the tragedy occurred. "The Cuban said that since he was drunk he couldn't hear any shots, and he fell asleep quickly. My daughter was found in the bathroom with her hand in the toilet bowl and a bullet wound in her neck," she said.

The dead woman is survived by two children, 2 and 3, from her previous marriage. The revolver with which the young woman was killed was owned by the Cuban and was sent to Managua in connection with the investigations. "But I suspect that my daughter did not commit suicide as they would have me believe. They have told me nothing about the investigations they are supposedly conducting in Managua. There is even a rumor that the Cuban is free and that at any moment he will be sent back to his country, while I have to think about supporting my two grandchildren," Mrs. Enríquez said finally. (See Appendix D for other examples of censorship.)

As 1985 ended, the Sandinista campaign against *La Prensa* had reached rabid levels. No epithet was too vile, no accusation was too fantastic to use in their sustained war against the independent opposition.

And yet there was a kind of totalitarian appropriateness in the way they degraded language and trivialized thought. For instance, to the Sandinistas a Contra is anyone against the "revolutionary process"; a Contra is anyone who questions the government; a Contra is anyone indifferent or neutral to state-manipulated hysteria—the whole insane litany of spies, conspiracies, traitors, CIA agents, and the corrupt bourgeoisie. In the dark interstices of the Sandinista mind, almost everyone is potentially a Contra or a CIA agent. As they huffed and puffed blowing up cardboard parodies of Somocista fascists and the big bogey man from the North, they became prisoners of their self-fulfilling rhetoric, resembling and sounding like the ferocious imperialists of their fantasies. How often Somoza had accused us of being Communist agents, and so as the Sandinistas turned into their own language, who did they resemble more than Anastasio Somoza himself—puffed up and magnified into the nightmare that afflicted and inspired their haunted imaginations.

Forty-three years of *Somocismo* had transfixed the Sandinista soul. In a perverse paradox where left becomes right, they copied what they secretly admired, turning the *Nicolasa* into the *turbas divinas*, and swaggering around with protruding pistols—as Tomás Borge did when he unwittingly imitated Somoza, illustrating repeatedly the dark nexus between *Somocismo* and *Sandinismo*. They copied Castro of course. He was the other side of their turbulent schizophrenic souls, the other side of their reactionary ideology yearning to be the "other"—the fascist monster who also turned into its inverted mirror image, dragging the blinding glass across each other's eyes. Children of a bastard ideology, they had come to slay the monster, but in the end they became a new monster that even the old monster feared to dream.

Silence—and the Revolution Within

THE SANDINISTAS OPENED 1986 by closing *Radio Católica*, the penultimate independent voice in Nicaragua.

On 14 January 1986 the government censored a *La Prensa* editorial congratulating the Guatemalan people for the restoration of democracy in Guatemala and another editorial welcoming the Spanish foreign minister to Nicaragua. (See Appendix E for examples of censorship in 1986.) Our reporters remained banned from the war zone while the reporters of *Barricada* and *El Nuevo Diario* were busy investigating human rights violations by the Contras. On 2 March an interview with Pablo Antonio Cuadra was partially censored in *La Prensa Literaria*. (See Appendix F.) The photo and name of Cardinal Obando y Bravo were not permitted. On 7 April we could not publish because of excessive censorship. The censorship figures, rounded off, for the first four months were 58 percent, 32 percent, 58 percent, and 46 percent. In addition, the time the censor had used for reviewing and "revising" our submitted materials had risen from two hours in 1982 to the absurd level of eight to nine hours in the months leading up to June. Of course, the delays were intentional, especially as we were ordered by the government to submit and publish only six pages daily. Before the triumph of the Revolution, *La Prensa* had averaged thirty-five pages.

In addition, knowing that its discriminatory policies were damaging our newspaper, the government's deliberate actions were orchestrated to bankrupt us. For instance, the time and material spent to fulfill censorship requirements raised our production costs more than 20 percent.

As though this problem were not sufficient, the government, as of 1 January 1986, ordered a 100 percent increase in salaries (the government controls salaries in Nicaragua) for *La Prensa* employees; a few days later the national currency was devalued 250 percent, causing a proportional increase in the price of paper and other costs. At the same time, we were denied, during a three-month period, permission to raise the price of *La Prensa*, so there was no way we could compensate for these additional costs. Another blow fell on 7 February, when we were ordered to reduce our weekly number of pages from sixty-eight to thirty-six, thus automatically reducing our advertising revenues by 50 percent.

Struggling against this tangle of economic problems that the government itself had created, we were then ordered to reduce our circulation because the Sandinistas claimed they could no longer obtain the foreign currency to purchase the paper needed to print the newspaper. Hence we were also confronted with the difficulty of obtaining foreign currency from the government to pay for the imported raw materials needed by *La Prensa* in addition to any donated materials. (Even when we had been able to obtain foreign currency from the *Casa de Cambio*, authorized by the government, we were charged a rate of twelve and a half times higher than what the Sandinista newspapers were charged.) The calculated lack of paper, controlled and stringently rationed by the government, caused us immense difficulties. For a time, *La Prensa* had been allowed to publish twelve-page editions, but as of February 1986, the quota was reduced to six. (The government received paper, which it then sold, from the Soviet Union.)

To remedy the situation, some members of Inter-American Press Association (IAPA) made an offer in April 1986 to supply *La Prensa* with paper free of charge, but on one condition: the Sandinistas had to guarantee that the gift would be used as a supplement to *La Prensa*'s regular allotment, so that the newspaper could come out in larger editions. Needless to say, the Sandinistas refused to make this guarantee. They made it clear that if *La Prensa* accepted the donation, the government would not feel obligated to supply any paper at all, and would deduct what the IAPA supplied from *La Prensa*'s regular allotment. In a letter to me dated 29 April, René Núñez, one of the government ministers, warned that even if it did get additional paper, *La Prensa* would still be limited to six pages. We had no choice, therefore, but to decline the generous offer.

In the midst of struggling with threats, censorship, and the exorbitant losses caused directly by the Sandinista government, we were confronted with another attempt to take over *La Prensa*. On 11 April 1986 Xavier Chamorro, editor of *El Nuevo Diario*, suddenly made an offer to buy *La Prensa* for a substantial amount of U.S. dollars. We were talking in the living room of my house during a family reunion, when Xavier made the offer. I had the distinct impression that the Sandinistas had decided to finish *La Prensa* and the easiest way to do it was through Xavier's services. Xavier told me that he was worried about my personal security and seemed to be implying that it would be better if I agreed to accept his offer before the Sandinistas confiscated *La Prensa* and something "happened" to me. Of course, both *La Prensa*'s employees and its board of directors categorically rejected this offer, suspecting immediately that the Sandinistas were behind it.

What better way, after all, to solve their image problem than by acquiring *La Prensa* and turning it into a puppet newspaper that would be mildly critical of the government, but not on fundamental issues? Then they could eliminate the cumbersome machinery of censorship and tell the world there is a free press in Nicaragua. Apart from the trickery involved, we were also personally offended by the Sandinista offer, for essentially it was an offer to sell out our ideas and values and thus betray the history and struggle of *La Prensa* and the memory of its murdered editor—whose words had been banned from the paper by the Sandinista censor ever since 1982.

When the Sandinista government closed *Radio Católica* on 1 January 1986, we felt that our turn would be next. Then when the Sandinistas made their "offer" to buy the paper we sensed that something definitive was about to happen. On 25 June, the U.S. House of Representatives voted $100 million in military and humanitarian aid to the Contras. The Sandinistas quickly made this their pretext.

On 26 June 1986 the government closed *La Prensa*. We received a short, three-line letter from Nelba Blandón: "By way of superior instructions, I notify you that from here on the newspaper *La Prensa* is indefinitely closed." Then the avalanche of lies began.

The two Sandinista newspapers, *Barricada* and *El Nuevo Diario*, obediently published the ominous order from the Media Office, as well as the government's justification. The following government communiqué was sent to us and appeared in *Barricada* and *El Nuevo Diario* on 27 June:

La Prensa Suspended
SANCTIONS FOR VIOLATIONS OF THE EMERGENCY LAW NOTICE

The Communications Media Office of the Ministry of Interior announces to the Nicaraguan People:

1. Whereas the immoral approval of the $100 million on the part of the North American administration for the counterrevolutionary forces means the continuation of the war of aggression, now already declared, which inside our country has been stimulated, defended, and even more, arranged by some anti-patriotic sectors;

2. Whereas inasmuch as our people strengthens its forces to confront and defeat the imperialist aggression, which has meant death and destruction in the Nicaraguan population, the *La Prensa* newspaper, acting as spokesman for the aggressive power, has been raising its levels of provocation, disinformation, pretending with it to justify the North American aggression, denying the validity of the *Contadora* Group as the only possible solution to achieve peace in Central America;

3. Whereas *La Prensa* has not at any time fulfilled its social, ethical, and professional responsibility, nor has it acted as a reflection of the common objectives of Nicaraguan society, which as a news medium is its obligation to the people;

4. Whereas it has repeatedly violated and shown disrespect for the directives issued by this Office, reproducing and spreading items expressly not authorized;

5. Whereas despite the preventive warnings made to the *La Prensa* editors, they continued in their attitude of contempt and disturbance of Public Security and Peace;

6. Whereas in view of all the above and based on Decree #130 of October 31, 1985 and on Articles #1, #2 and #3 of the *Provisional General Law on the Communications Media* and Articles #42, #43, and #46 of the Regulations of the same Law, this Office resolves to indefinitely suspend the editions of the *La Prensa* newspaper;

Given in the city of Managua, on the twenty-sixth day of the month of June, 1986.

In this communiqué and subsequent government pronouncements, the Sandinista government tried to justify its arbitrary action by basing it on the U.S. Congress's vote. It is sufficient to observe that neither *La Prensa* nor anyone else in Nicaragua could participate in a decision by an independent body that attends to the fundamental interests of its country. Hence to link the vote in the U.S. Congress with the closing of *La Prensa* was only the latest pretext to consolidate a totalitarian political system hostile and alien to the Nicaraguan people.

Confronted with the fact that *La Prensa* did not vote in the U.S. Congress, the Sandinistas produced another lie. They asserted that before the vote, *La Prensa* owners, specifically Violeta Barrios de Chamorro and myself, were in Washington lobbying for aid to the Contras. We were in Washington, but we did not "lobby" for aid.

Our visit corresponded exclusively to an invitation from a group of Democratic and Republican Congressmen and other distinguished persons who had invited us to a dinner to discuss the situation of *La Prensa*.

Our appearance was covered in the U.S. media, so the record speaks for itself. For instance, an Associated Press (AP) dispatch carried in many papers throughout the United States on 26 May reported the following:

> The dinner was held in honor of Mr. Chamorro and his sister-in-law, Violeta de Chamorro, the publisher of *La Prensa*. Most of the more than 100 people in attendance were affiliated with the Democratic Party.
>
> While criticizing the Sandinistas, neither of the Chamorros took a position on the $100 million aid request for the Contra rebels pending before the U.S. Congress.
>
> Mrs. Chamorro, however, said, "Without liberty, there will never be peace!"

What Violeta and I did say on this occasion was published in a pamphlet entitled "Without Liberty First, There Will Never Be Peace." In her presentation, Violeta cited a letter she had written to the presidents of the *Contadora* countries, stressing that the *Contadora* Act should give equal importance to the removal of foreign advisors and to the public liberties of the oppressed Nicaraguan people. She added that if the Act was signed and its provisions complied with, then "The Republic of Nicaragua for which my husband died would be realized." She ended by saying that the following "is the position" of *La Prensa* "with regard to the Central American crisis":

If, on the other hand, this act is not signed by the FSLN or is signed but not complied with, Nicaragua will keep on destroying itself, our youth will keep dying, and the danger of violent confrontation in Nicaragua will increase. Those responsible for this will not only be the nine comandantes, but all of Latin America.

Ironically, Violeta's comments followed the line of the banned 26 June issue of *La Prensa*. In the editorial, *La Prensa* stated that aid voted for the Contras would quickly increase anguish, hunger, and death and that *La Prensa* supported the *Contadora* process.

Indeed, the Sandinista communiqué's reference to the *Contadora* process was the height of hypocrisy, for *La Prensa* had supported a verifiable *Contadora* solution from the beginning, while the government had systematically censored our news and editorials in support of *Contadora*. In contrast, the Sandinistas invoked the *Contadora* process to buy time. It was clear by 1985 that, with all the contending interests and tensions, the *Contadora* process was going nowhere. But the Sandinistas paid lip service to it because, to them, it was a vehicle to delay or deter sustained military action against their regime. By censoring *La Prensa* editorials, they revealed again how censorship can be used to create an image: for, after all, they could claim that we never supported *Contadora* —there was no "record."

Point three of the communiqué harkens back to the tendentious *General Provisional Law on the Media of Communication* decreed in 1979. Thus "social, ethical, and professional responsibility" and the "reflection of the common objectives of Nicaraguan society" were completely contingent on whatever the government arbitrarily decided they were or were not: as always with the Sandinistas, saying it made it so.

The most colossal lie, the most egregious example of Sandinista hypocrisy, however, appears in point two of the communiqué: "The *La Prensa* newspaper" had acted as "spokesman" for the interests of the "aggressive power"—increased its provocations, its "disinformation"—pretending to "justify the North American aggression." Indeed, this was the principal Sandinista line repeated over the world and by Daniel Ortega in the "aggressor's" homeland: *La Prensa* was a spokesman for the Reagan administration, the paid voice of the CIA.

Now, we at *La Prensa* have a fundamental question for the Sandinistas and their supporters: since *La Prensa* had to submit daily to strict and systematic *prior* censorship ever since March 1982, how could it be a "spokesman" for anybody, let alone the United States and its intelligence agencies? Perhaps our sinister "subliminal" messages again destabilized the censors causing them to overlook articles, editorials, and secret codes enthusiastically supporting Reagan administration policies, supporting CIA aggression, supporting the Contras, etc. But since, as opposed to censorship by omission, there is a "record," let them now show the *La Prensa* issues in which we were spokesmen for foreign interests. They cannot. Moreover, they cannot pretend that all these articles, editorials, and news items were censored, for then they commit one of their many contradictions: one cannot be silenced and at the same time be a "voice" or "spokesman." No, the Sandinistas will have to do better than this.

We will try to help them. Let us imagine that we did submit pro-Reagan, pro-CIA, pro-Contra propaganda, or anything else the most bizarre left-wing fantasy can devise, to prior censorship. First, this would have been completely suicidal on our part; second, it would have placed on a silver platter the fantasized evidence, the proof that all their lies were true! They would then have allowed *La Prensa* to publish one issue and then definitively closed it for being a "destabilizing" threat to "national security" and all those other terrible things they accused it of being.

There is one more detail related to the government's closing of *La Prensa*, even though it is not specifically mentioned in the 27 June communiqué. On 3 April 1986 the *Washington Post* published an Op Ed article I had written entitled "Don't Abandon the Nicaraguan People." My central point was that if the Sandinistas converted Nicaragua into a center for continental subversion, then sooner or later the United States would see its security threatened and have to take military actions that could be disastrous for the American continent. The Sandinistas later used this article to justify the closing of *La Prensa* to the Organization of American States' (OAS) Inter-American Commission on Human Rights.

Two things need to be pointed out. First, I wrote the article in my capacity as a private individual; I gave my personal opinion and not that of *La Prensa*. As a person identified with the many people and parties that oppose the Sandinistas inside Nicaragua, I consider it a human right to be able to express my personal opinion freely. Second, there is a distinction between myself as an individual and *La Prensa* as an institution. It is pertinent to remember that in the times of Somoza, Pedro Joaquín organized an armed invasion against the government, but *La Prensa* was not closed.

The reason the Sandinistas did not close *La Prensa* before 26 June is precisely because they did not have any plausible pretext to close us. They huffed and puffed about *El Mercurio*, subliminal messages, CIA funding, and a host of other lies and slanders, but they blew nothing down. Moreover, for a while, they needed *La Prensa* to show the world that they were democratic, that there was pluralism in Nicaragua, because there was an opposition newspaper. We, in a sense, helped legitimize them, helped them to gain Western credits and aid that still inexplicably continue to flow into their bankrupt economy. At that time, there was a perceived political cost for closing *La Prensa*. But then they noticed something that all their mentors have noticed: many political activists and influential organizations in the free world seem to use a double standard when pressuring dictatorships of the left as distinguished from the right. The difference for us was telling. How we remember the international support we received when Somoza censored or closed us. There was an incessant cry of outrage from governments and other international bodies. Sustained world opinion contributed to freedom in Nicaragua. But as a dictatorship of the left, the Sandinistas did not have to worry about this; they merely had to proclaim a lie to make it officially true.

After we were closed, our immediate concern was for *La Prensa*'s workers and their families. We had 230 employees, and we continued to pay their full salaries as long as we could. Many Nicaraguans generously helped us by continuing to pay their subscriptions, and some of the independent political parties contributed what money they could. But this was not enough, and so as we began to sell equipment and trucks to keep our employees on the payroll and as our dwindling resources began to disappear, we were forced to lay off 119 of our employees, on 31 August 1986. On 3 September *La Prensa* employees, through their union, asked Daniel Ortega to reopen *La Prensa*. The request was ignored. By 3 March 1987, only fifty-three employees remained on the payroll. The closing of *La Prensa* thus constituted an immense personal tragedy for our employees—a tragedy exacerbated by the fact that there is now more hunger and poverty in Nicaragua than at any time in its history. Thus the Sandinista government, supposed defender of the workers, bears responsibility for the suffering of those they have deprived of their right to make a living. (It should be noted that after the Sandinista government closed *La Prensa*, the Ministry of Labor repeatedly ordered us to continue paying our employees in full, even after we had run out of money and were selling trucks and equipment. The arrogant hypocrisy of the Sandinistas' strategy was blatantly obvious: they wanted to ensure our bankruptcy even though they themselves were responsible for what had happened. In addition, it was impossible for *La Prensa* employees to find work in state agencies because the state owns and controls practically everything in Nicaragua. Their *La Prensa* affiliation constituted a "black mark" against them. Consequently, many had to leave the country.)

In the meantime, we had appealed the government's closing to the Supreme Court on 28 June, and, on 25 September, the Court predictably upheld the government's action. But it was apparently inadequately "independent": in December 1987, Daniel Ortega asked the entire Supreme Court to resign and then submitted his own candidates to the National Assembly for approval. In addition, the government intensified its rhetoric of aggression against *La Prensa* owners.

On 19 July 1986, on the seventh anniversary of the revolution's triumph, the president of Nicaragua, Daniel Ortega, made a public speech before a crowd estimated at 10,000. The speech was mandatorily transmitted by all radio and television throughout Nicaragua. In his speech, Comandante Ortega accused us and particularly Violeta, in our capacities as *La Prensa* owners, of being criminals who deserved to be tried by "the People's Anti-Somocista Tribunals" and sentenced to thirty years in prison for "betraying the country." Somoza had, of course, made the same accusations.

In an open letter to Comandante Ortega that could not be published in Nicaragua, Violeta replied as follows:

President Ortega,

As chairman of the board of directors of *La Prensa*, I was not greatly astonished to hear your recent statement that I deserve to be sentenced to 30 years in jail after being tried by the people's anti-Somocista tribunals.

I say that I listened to these words without surprise, because I am now accustomed to hearing you speak. Your expression is confused and contradictory, full of the kinds of passion not befitting a head of state.

If you so desire, I will happily turn myself in to the authorities, so that they may apply the jail sentence with which you are threatening me. In this way, I will be proudly following the example of my husband, Pedro Joaquín Chamorro Cardenal. Imprisonment was the only way the previous dictatorship, led by Gen. Anastasio Somoza Debayle, could deal with him. If perhaps my age or the precarious state of my health does not permit me to serve the 30-year sentence you want for me, then you can easily follow the example set for the American spy who betrayed his country, which you mentioned in your speech, and apply two life sentences plus 50 or 60 years, if that appeals to you.

How quickly you have forgotten my strong nationalist position. Remember that in 1979, in San José, Costa Rica, I was the only one who opposed any resolution of the Nicaraguan problem that included the involvement of foreign countries. What I said then I say now: the grave crisis afflicting Nicaragua must be resolved among ourselves, the Nicaraguans, without the interference of Cubans, Soviets, or Americans.

You will never convince anyone that I am a traitor to my country, nor that I received money from the Central Intelligence Agency, nor that I am part of the Reagan Administration's terrorist plan. These falsehoods have been repeated so often that now nobody believes them. Comandante Ortega, the same thing is happening here in Nicaragua as in other countries under Communist dictatorships: because there are so many lies every day, no one will believe you on the day when you say something true.

I also heard in your speech that you seem to like the idea of doing with me what the Americans did with the citizens of Japanese descent during the greatest armed conflict in history: imprison everyone who is slightly suspicious in concentration camps.

This is already under way, Comandante Ortega, by means of repression and the banning of all opposition opinion. Your Sandinista party has already created a great concentration camp in Nicaragua. But the Nicaraguan people are not losing their liberating spirit and will never lose it even in the worst of the gulags your mind is able to conceive.

On Wednesday 6 August 1986, Sandinista police broke up a demonstration in front of *La Prensa* by members of the Social Christian party, who were calling for our newspaper's reopening. Afterwards the police did not intervene as more than 100 members of a Sandinista union also held a demonstration in front of *La Prensa*—painting black and red slogans and insults and Sandinista emblems on the walls of *La Prensa*.

They also burned the Nicaraguan flag and the flags of *La Prensa* and the Vatican. Many of these demonstrators arrived in government trucks and were waved at by Sandinista police in a jeep that drove past *La Prensa*.

On 9 January 1987, the Sandinista government released its new constitution with much pomp and ceremony. One hour later, President Daniel Ortega suspended it due to the "state of national emergency." As our Board of Directors had intended to reopen *La Prensa* under the protection of the constitution (specifically Title IV, Article 29; Chapter III, Articles #67 and #68), Violeta de Chamorro sent a letter on 9 January to the government informing it that *La Prensa* planned to begin publication. This letter was not answered, and thus she sent an issue of *La Prensa* on 16 January for the government's approval. She then received a note from Subcomandante Raúl Cordón Morice, the new, temporary head of the censorship office. Cordón replied, à la Nelba Blandón, that "by superior instructions, said newspaper is not authorized to circulate."

La Prensa's 61st anniversary on 2 March 1987 was passed in silence. On 30 April 1987, Sandinista security agents, under the command of Capt. Oscar Loza, forcibly occupied *La Prensa* for four hours. They detained several *La Prensa* employees, including the directors, interrogating them and threatening them with jail for distributing leaflets addressed to members of the World Interparliamentary Union who were meeting in Managua. The leaflets carried the *La Prensa* logo and had a photo of Pedro Joaquín Chamorro Cardenal in the background. The leaflets asked the members to support freedom of the press in Nicaragua. Several delegations arrived at *La Prensa* to express support. A French delegation arrived while the security agents were inside and was turned away. Four hours later the security force withdrew, after searching the entire building and seizing the leaflets and materials used to print them, including plates, film, and all of the copies of a pamphlet we had presented to the Organization of American States responding to the Sandinista government's justification for *La Prensa*'s closure. Nelba Blandón, now a spokeswoman for the Ministry of Interior, promised "pertinent investigations" of *La Prensa*. On 26 June 1987, one year after *La Prensa* had been closed, Sandinista police broke up a demonstration by *La Prensa* employees and a group of opposition politicians and businessmen on behalf of a free press. The police tore down assorted posters protesting Sandinista censorship.

In August 1987 Sandinista security police arrested numerous journalists who had been denounced by the pro-Sandinista Union of Nicaraguan Journalists (UPN), which had accused them of transmitting information to "counterrevolutionary" radio stations in the exterior. Many of the journalists were interrogated and threatened in the notorious Casa 50. Among them were various journalists who had worked for *La Prensa*, including Fidelina Suárez, Alejandro Cordonero, Enrique García, and other journalists that did not work at *La Prensa* such as Julio Armas and Róger León Carranza. UPN also denounced and accused several secretaries who work for opposition political parties. This was merely the latest episode the government has contrived to intimidate the remaining independent journalists—journalists who have no access to the media in or outside Nicaragua. For months the government had made ominous warnings about the dreaded "ideological penetration of the enemy" in an effort to translate its proficiency in murdering people to murdering ideas.

On 7 August 1987 the Sandinista government co-signed a regional peace plan in Guatemala with the governments of Costa Rica, El Salvador, Honduras, and Guatemala. According to that plan, the Sandinistas must open a political space in Nicaragua, allowing pluralism and democratic opposition. On Saturday 19 September 1987 at the prompting of the visiting Costa Rican foreign minister, Rodrigo Madrigal Nieto, a longtime friend of our family, Daniel Ortega met with Violeta in her house to explore the possibility of opening *La Prensa*. Ortega tried to get Violeta to agree to limited censorship, as did Jaime Wheelock, the Sandinista agrarian reform minister, when he visited Violeta later that day. Violeta's response was the same in both cases: either *La Prensa* could publish with complete press freedom or we would not publish. The meeting with Ortega lasted approximately four hours, and he finally agreed to allow *La Prensa* to publish without any censorship whatsoever. The paper's directors made it clear then and subsequently that we would cease publishing immediately if the government reimposed any kind of censorship and broke the Guatemala accord which stipulated complete press freedom by 7 November 1987. Since the Sandinistas know this, any imposition of state censorship will, in effect, constitute the intentional closure of *La Prensa*.

During the meeting, Comandante Ortega and other government officials promised that we would have access to newsprint and guaranteed that those who worked in *La Prensa* would not be harassed or harmed—in contrast to what has happened in the past.

Both the government and *La Prensa's* directors issued a joint communiqué stating that *La Prensa* would be able to publish without any restrictions except those imposed by the exercise of "responsible journalism." In addition, there was another document—the "minutes" of all that transpired in the meeting in Violeta's house. This was not published. Among the points agreed on in this document was the Sandinistas' recognition that previous censorship of *La Prensa* was excessive and illogical.

Despite the government announcement on September 19, we were unable to publish until 1 October, 1987, due to broken equipment that was being repaired and the need to reorganize our personnel. As most of our employees had been forced to leave the country, we had to manage with only a skeleton crew, which included only four reporters, two editors, and one photographer. In addition, although *La Prensa* was quickly sold out once it hit the streets, we still lacked the vehicles, which were earlier sold to support our employees, to distribute *La Prensa* widely (we had to subsequently rent transportation from other sources).

In our 1 October edition, Violeta Chamorro insisted that *La Prensa* should not be the privileged exception; she insisted that all the Nicaraguan media should be free. So far this has not happened. As this book went to press, it was doubtful whether the Sandinistas would live up to the agreement they signed 7 August 1987. By July 1988, they had not complied with most of the Guatemala accords.

In early September, Cruz Flores, a *La Prensa* photographer, was arrested at his home and taken to Casa 50 at three o'clock in the morning. On 15 August Flores had taken photos of Sandinista police attacking approximately 1,000 people who were preparing to hold a march after inaugurating a new headquarters of the Nicaraguan Democratic Coordinating Board (CDN)—an umbrella group of opponents of the Sandinista government. The police used riot sticks, electric prods, and German shepherds to break up the march, and they arrested at least ten people, including Lino Hernández, executive secretary of Nicaragua's Permanent Commission on Human Rights (CPDH) and Alberto Saborío, head of the Nicaraguan Bar Association and the secretary general of the Nicaraguan Conservative Party. This happened just eight days after the Sandinistas had signed the peace accord guaranteeing democracy. The Sandinista police confiscated Flores's film and when he was later arrested, he was locked for hours in a room with freezing temperatures. He was then interrogated about the activities of *La Prensa*'s board of directors and the remaining *La Prensa* employees. During his interrogation by three Sandinista officials, they ostentatiously laid their pistols on the table, insinuating that he could be killed at any moment. He was finally released twelve hours later.

On 22 October 1987 Carlos Ampié Calero, a *La Prensa* reporter, was asked by a group of men if he worked for *La Prensa*. When he answered "yes," he was told that *La Prensa* "had passed the line" and that the Revolution would not permit it. He was then beaten. On 2 November, Comandante Bayardo Arce accused *La Prensa* of publishing "grotesque lies," but, as usual, he failed to specify the "lies."

In Washington, on 11 November, Daniel Ortega declared that *La Prensa* and *Radio Católica* would be closed if the U.S. Congress voted additional aid to the Contras. Ortega was, in effect, threatening to hold the two selected symbols of freedom in Nicaragua hostage to U.S. foreign policy. It was blatant, political blackmail. On the same day, 11 November, a *La Prensa* vendor, Etelvína Diaz, was threatened by a Sandinista supporter, formerly an enthusiastic Somocista, who had previously disrupted *La Prensa* sales.

On 14 November, Guillermo Amador, a *La Prensa* distributor, was captured by a Sandinista patrol headed by Lt. Victor Mairena. Amador's wife suspects that her husband was denounced by Bernardo Torres, a CDS activist. On 17 November, three *La Prensa* news carriers were beaten by Sandinista police after they reported the robbery of a large quantity of newspapers.

In Bluefields, early December 1987, a *La Prensa* newsboy, thirteen-year-old Sergio Navas Sálomon, was sought by State Security. While selling *La Prensa*, Navas Sálomon had shouted the news about a Cuban who had killed a young girl in Bluefields. Indeed, Navas Sálomon, whose father is a *La Prensa* distributor, had shouted, "Cuban kills Nicaraguan girl" as well as "Nicaragua for the Nicaraguans" and "Cubans go home." The last two phrases undoubtably added insult to injury, and hence Lt. Hector Wilson, head of state security in Bluefields, ordered the boy's arrest. But when he could not be found the security force arrested an older brother and, in effect, held him hostage. Lt. Wilson told a family lawyer that Navas Sálomon was being sought by state security for committing "ideological diversionism."

On 10 January 1988, 15,000 Nicaraguans took to the streets to honor the memory of Pedro Joaquín Chamorro and to protest Sandinista repression.

On 18 January, *El Nuevo Diario* personally attacked Violeta de Chamorro in the form of a "joke" that suggested that her husband had been murdered because she was trying to hide a love affair. In addition, Violeta has recently been subjected to another campaign of insulting, obscene phone calls at late hours.

Moreover, between February and March, the Sandinista TV network ran a "commercial" showing footage of Violeta, Pablo Antonio Cuadra, and myself interwoven with scenes of suffering war victims—clearly suggesting that *La Prensa* is responsible for Contra attacks. In one scene, children are shown who had been killed in a bus that hit a mine, and then Violeta is shown saying goodbye to Jeane Kirkpatrick as she leaves *La Prensa*. As Violeta thanks her guest for the visit, the word "gracias" is used to suggest that she is grateful for the children's deaths. Even by Sandinista standards this vile campaign of vilification is unprecedented. (In June 1988, the Sandinista media showed the bullet-ridden body of Violeta's husband [Pedro Joaquín Chamorro Cardenal] next to photographs and/or videos of herself—suggesting that she was pleased that Pedro had been murdered. [See Appendix G.])

On 3 March the government transported hundreds of government workers to *La Prensa*, producing a staged show of predictable accusations and slogans.

On 23 March the Sandinista government and the Nicaraguan Resistance signed a ceasefire agreement in the Nicaraguan town of Sapoá. The treaty eventually envisions the Contras reincorporating themselves into the political opposition inside Nicaragua once the democratization of the country is determined to be irreversible. Point #5 of the agreement guarantees "unrestricted freedom of expression as contemplated in the Accord of Esquipulus II," signed 7 August in Guatemala.

Precisely because the Sandinistas have not complied with the Guatemala accord, we doubt that they will comply with either the letter or the spirit of the Sapoá agreement. The Sandinistas' record clearly indicates the opposite. During February and March the government again unleashed the *turbas* against the opposition; Socialist union leaders supporting strikes have been forcibly drafted into the army, and an old law has been reactivated and used to sentence defendants for crimes against "public order."

In regard to "unrestricted" press freedom, the Sandinistas continue to openly violate both the Guatemala and the Sapoá accords. They have publicly declared that they will not permit any independent TV station; and they have indefinitely closed one radio station and banned several news programs.

On 29 April Tomás Borge, the minister of interior, physically attacked José Castillo Osejo, director of *Radio Corporación*—bloodying his face. On 16 May 1988, Lt. Lissette Torres, chief of the Interior Ministry's Media Office, threatened to close the few independent radio stations that were broadcasting news about the military draft and the country's economic crisis.

In addition, numerous recent events reinforce our doubts about Sandinista promises. On 20 March 1988, Violeta Barrios de Chamorro, in a report given to the InterAmerican Press Association in the Dominican Republic, accused the Sandinistas of the following activities: employing a military official who makes frequent "anonymous" phone calls reminding us that we are "human beings" and can be killed; using a high government functionary, with the rank of minister, to warn us that they will unleash a "personal war" against Violeta to destroy her "morally" if *La Prensa* continues "the same line"; in the same way, threatening people who publish denunciations or complaints in our paper; imprisoning Juan Carlos Corea, a *La Prensa* journalist, and beating him for covering a news event; using State Security to verbally threaten Fidelina Suárez, another of our journalists. Violeta also points out that people encouraged by the government continue to destroy stacks of *La Prensa* in the streets, in the presence of our defenseless agents and newsboys. Moreover, the government continues to mount "*turba* shows" in front of our offices in the presence of Sandinista police—thus giving these acts of intimidation an implicit state sanction.

Violeta notes that on at least four occasions since the signing of the Guatemala peace plan, Daniel Ortega and the FSLN have issued direct threats against *La Prensa*.

Six more recent events illustrate why we remain skeptical of Sandinista promises. Since October 1987, we had been asking the government for more newsprint, knowing that our restricted supply was contingent on what the government decided to sell us. On 17 October we had also requested permission to buy $15,000 worth of foreign currency in order to purchase the raw materials and the mechanical equipment necessary to publish. The government, through Comandante Jaime Wheelock, authorized the *Casa de Cambio* to sell us the foreign currency at a rate of 20,000 to one. But after this date there were no further authorizations for foreign currency until April 1988—six months later. Since December the government had not sold us newsprint, despite repeated requests. Consequently, by late March we were running out of paper and hence in April we could not publish for four days (6-9 April) because we had no newsprint.

The pertinent point is that Daniel Ortega had personally promised us that the government would supply us sufficient quantities of newsprint. He made that promise on 19 September as part of the agreement under which *La Prensa* would reopen. Thus the Sandinista government has violated this agreement as well as the agreements signed in Guatemala and Sapoá guaranteeing unrestricted press freedom.

In April, the government's excuse was that it had run out of paper: a Soviet ship carrying supplies to Nicaragua had been delayed. During this period, however, *El Nuevo Diario* and *Barricada* continued to publish, averaging between twelve and sixteen pages daily. We had earlier suspended publication of *La Prensa Literaria* and sports supplements; we did not publish on Sundays and had reduced our circulation, so we could save paper. The two Sandinista newspapers, in contrast, continued issuing extra editions and various supplements in excess of public demand.

If the government had no newsprint, how could *Barricada* and *El Nuevo Diario* continue publishing unless the government was discriminating against *La Prensa*—which it was. When queried by the international media about this discrepancy, the government claimed that the Sandinista newspapers were using newsprint donated by the Soviet Communist party. Why then does the Sandinista government continue to deny *La Prensa* similar paper donations from democratic institutions—in addition to controlling the foreign currency needed to purchase raw materials and the approval to send or receive anything at all? On 8 April government Ministry of Industry officials suddenly remembered that eighty tons of newsprint stockpiled since 1984 by the Electoral Council were available to be sold to all Nicaraguan newspapers.

On 15 April 1988, approximately 300 members of Juventud Sandinista, a Sandinista youth group, pelted *La Prensa* with rocks and shouted Sandinista slogans.

On 7 July 1988, Bayardo Arce, a member of the Sandinista National Directorate, declared in a speech that United States diplomats were "organizing the pages of *La Prensa* and even writing its editorials." This preposterous lie made us suspect that the Sandinistas had decided to violate, even more blatantly, the accords signed in Guatemala and Sapoá.

On 10 July, Sandinista police brutally broke up an opposition rally in Nandaime, Nicaragua that had been authorized by the government.

Scores of armed police attacked with rifle butts, truncheons, and tear gas—injuring and arresting many attending the rally.

On 11 July the Sandinista government indefinitely closed *Radio Católica* for reporting on the attack—mendaciously accusing it of inciting "violence"—and Lieutenant Lissette Torres, chief of the Interior Ministry's Media Office, threatened to close *Radio Corporación* if it did not modify the tone of its news programs.

Finally, on the same day, 11 July 1988, *La Prensa* was closed by the government for fifteen days—the pretext was the same used against *Radio Católica*. Thus we were forced back to square one. We now believe that the Sandinistas have no intention of complying with the peace accords and have been using them only for tactical and propaganda purposes. Hence the closings are especially revealing because the government had show-cased the opening of *Radio Católica* and *La Prensa* as "examples" of its willingness to allow a democratic opposition to exist within Sandinista Nicaragua.

Hence we at *La Prensa* again reaffirm our solidarity with all the oppressed people of Nicaragua: the workers, peasants, merchants; the thousands of political prisoners, especially those outside Managua; the anguished mothers and fathers, the Miskito Indians, the restricted political parties and labor unions; the media that are censored or closed, the repressed churches; in short—all the suffering people of Nicaragua.

We believe that freedom is indivisible and that we are linked to each other in a common destiny: we know that temporary freedom for some ends in total oppression for everyone. Thus we ask free men and women to look carefully at what is happening in Nicaragua and not to be distracted by short time frames or government spotlights shining on selected voices while others are silently suffocated in darkness. We, at *La Prensa,* are willing to test Sandinista words by their actions. We are aware that no Marxist-Leninist government has ever allowed itself to be genuinely tested in a democratic arena or has voluntarily abdicated power through a legitimate election. Thus if the Sandinistas continue the lie of censorship, confiscations, and closures—if they continue to inbreed within and through an alien and claustrophobic ideology, then they will perpetuate the suffocating nightmare of Marxist-Leninist regimes—the monster within the monster.

This is the pivotal moment in Nicaraguan history: the Sandinistas will either permit a pluralistic society to come into being—in which case they will cease being Marxist-Leninist—or they will use the peace plan to completely consolidate themselves in power, after which they will close all space and appropriate the air we breathe.

Epilogue

WHEN THE INSURRECTION against the Somoza dictatorship flamed up among the Nicaraguan people, we knew we were witnessing the beginning of the first authentic revolution in Latin America, a revolution that would create genuine freedom and justice. Even when we saw the revolution being betrayed, we knew its essential reality could never be extinguished, for each of us carried the revolution within us. This was the Sandinistas' fundamental, fatal error: they thought they could betray a dream and then murder it. But they can never censor, ban, or exile a revolution. They cannot murder a revolution rooted in the reality of a people's dreams and aspirations—a revolution that flowers daily in our hearts and minds.

Freedom is essentially revolutionary. And this is precisely why the Sandinistas are profoundly counterrevolutionary. Time is ultimately kind to a people whose destiny is freedom. As a people collectively renewed out of the imperishable blood and dreams of our ancestors, we cannot be forever silenced.

The Sandinistas can destroy radio stations; they can shut down newspapers; they can beat, imprison, exile, or murder whomever they choose—but ultimately they cannot silence the Nicaraguan people. They cannot censor our thoughts, they cannot imprison our hunger for freedom, they cannot exile our sense of justice. In the end, it is time itself that is against them. Not even the Sandinistas can censor, imprison, exile, or murder time—not even the monster can do that.

Managua, 14 July 1988.

Appendices

Appendix A

THIS IS THE article that appeared in *La Prensa* 29 July 1981, for which the newspaper was closed:

NICARAGUA ABSENT IN WEDDING
"We could have given them a hammock"

Nicaragua did not send an official delegation to the wedding of English Prince Charles, and was not represented by the new ambassador in London because he has not yet presented his credentials to the queen.

Francisco D'Escoto Brockman, Foreign Minister Miguel D'Escoto's brother, would have represented Nicaragua at the marvelous "fairy tale dream" nuptials of Charles of Wales and Lady Diana Spencer.

D'Escoto cannot be there because he won't be officially accredited before Queen Elizabeth II until next October, as scheduled by the Court of St. James.

According to our Foreign Office's spokesman, Nicaragua's ad-interim Chargé d'Affairs in London, Tomás Argüello, may participate in some of the events, but not in the most important ceremonies because he doesn't have the rank of ambassador.

The spokesman explained that Nicaragua has diplomatic relations with Great Britain and has received an invitation from the British government. However, he did not say if a present was sent to the royal couple. He explained that if a gift were sent, it wouldn't be anything like the one Mrs. Ronald Reagan presented from the United States (a Steuben glass vase valued at $70,000, but which Mrs. Reagan said she had bought for only $8,000).

"Where would we get the money to buy such things?" he asked, and in a light vein he remarked that we could have sent a Nicaraguan hammock for the royal couple's amusement.

In fact, official presents should be home products, and Nicaraguan craftsmen make many beautiful things that wouldn't be out of place in a king's wedding.

Finally, somebody suggested that, also for the amusement of the royal couple, we could have sent them a well-bound volume of Carlos Fonseca's *Works* as a wedding gift.

La Prensa, 7/29/81, p. 16.

Appendix B

"SANDINO: NATIONALIST BUT NEVER COMMUNIST"
by Pedro Joaquín Chamorro Cardenal

WHATEVER MAY BE said about him, Sandino is our country's greatest hero in modern times, and his memory should be kept with love in the heart of every Nicaraguan.

Sandino represents the rebelliousness of our people, and his glorious deeds in the Segovias mountains have given fame and prestige to Nicaragua throughout the world.

It is true that errors and injustices were committed during the war fought by Sandino, but those occur in every action of that nature, and the opposite faction, the one represented by the foreigners who exercised control over Nicaragua, also committed errors, injustices, and crimes.

It is not true, however, that Sandino was a Communist. He was a nationalist, which is different, and hundreds of testimonies prove it. Farabundo Martí spoke that truth when facing death by a firing squad in El Salvador. We could also add the historical fact, well known during Sandino's time, that Communists abhorred nationalism and directed their propaganda towards abolishing the very idea of "country."

Communists used to say that the idea of "country" was a bourgeois fabrication, and they still believe it, although they may no longer say it, because now they care more about advancing the political interests of the Soviet Union and spreading its doctrine than about their own country.

Sandino could not accept this internationalization that the Communists seek, because he was essentially a nationalist and a patriot—the very opposite of what Communists fundamentally are.

We should exalt Sandino's figure, precisely to confront the Communists, who obey interventionist directives from the Soviet Union and China.

Sandino fought the United States Marines, but he didn't bring Soviet cossacks to Nicaragua as Fidel Castro has done in Cuba.

There is a fundamental difference between Fidel Castro, who filled Cuba with Soviet rockets, soldiers, aircraft, and even canned goods, and Sandino who defended the sovereignty of his homeland with homemade bombs, without accepting patronage from any foreign power.

That is why Sandino was exceptional: instead of surrendering to foreign manipulation, he fought within the boundaries of an idealistic Indo-Hispanic world view.

Naturally, the Communists who attacked and slandered Sandino when he fought in the mountains are now trying to use him, because they have no ethics or shame to deter them in the use of anything, including what they have previously opposed—if it serves their purposes or lends prestige to their own propaganda.

Sandino was a pure product of our homeland, quite different from the products exported by the Soviet Union or China, and as such we must exalt his figure and preserve his memory.

The value of his deeds is purely Nicaraguan—not Soviet, and his nationalism is indigenous, not Russian.

Sandino is a monument to our country's dignity. We must not allow the Communists (whose beliefs he never held) to defile his memory by manipulating his prestige in order to turn our country over to the Soviet Union—under the pretext of fighting imperialism.

Appendix C

**LETTER BY VIOLETA BARRIOS DE CHAMORRO
SENT TO THE REVOLUTIONARY JUNTA, FEBRUARY 16, 1983**

Managua, February 16, 1983

Violeta B. de Chamorro

Señores
Members of the Junta
of the Government of National Reconstruction
Comandante of the Revolution Daniel Ortega Saavedra
Doctor Sergio Ramírez Mercado
Doctor Rafael Córdova Rivas
Managua

Esteemed Señores:
On the ninth of this month, I exercised my rights as a citizen and went to the offices of the Attorney General where I spoke to the vice-minister of justice, Dr. Boris Vega, and demanded the completion of the penal law still in effect and the promises that various comandantes of the Revolution have made to me on repeated occasions regarding the extradition of one of the convicted assassins [Silvio Vega] of my husband, who in life was known as Pedro Joaquín Chamorro Cardenal. Both the law and the promises guarantee the legal pursuit of those responsible for the planning, the management, and the payment for an assassination that ranks as one of the most repugnant political crimes in our continent's history.

As is natural, the newspaper *La Prensa* covered my visit objectively, as a legal matter. Nevertheless, we were surprised that censorship by the government over which you preside forced us either to cut parts of the article or suspend it completely. It is true that as we have become accustomed to censorship, this new example of the government's accelerated siege of press freedom in Nicaragua should not have astonished me—a fragile freedom for which my husband gave his life. In spite of this, I have an ineluctable obligation to protest respectfully but firmly the continual aggression against freedom of the press: a freedom guaranteed in the *Fundamental Statute*, in the Statute of *The Rights and Guarantees of the Nicaraguan People*, and in numerous other international accords that recognize freedom of the press as one of the most precious human rights, in addition to the *American Convention of Human Rights*, which is the law of this land.

In addition, I cannot be silent about the dolorous abuse of my husband's memory and the prohibition in *La Prensa* of his thoughts, his editorials, and his judgments: that is—Pedro Joaquín Chamorro Cardenal, a democrat who fought for Nicaragua's freedom and sacrificed his life for his country and the revolutionary triumph—is exiled from daily journalism and supplanted by opportunistic foreigners who abuse a Revolution that each day is removed further from its original principles.

In regard to the above, I write you to denounce the fact I mentioned at the beginning of this letter and to protest again the severe press censorship that is imposed with more vigor than censorship during the fatal days of the Somoza dynasty.

Finally, I want to tell you that I would like to believe that the government still has an interest in finding those truly guilty of the murder of my husband. It is sad to say but the Sandinista Court only condemned the assassins that had already been tried and processed in the last epoch of Somoza. Today, in the revolutionary period, the three judges who tried the case did not add one single new detail that was not discovered under Somoza.

Based on evidence from the Somoza trial, the guilty were sentenced. Unfortunately, five years after my husband's death, it seems that in the government sectors connected with the administration of justice, there is not the least interest in finding and punishing the assassins of Pedro, whose death detonated the patriotic avalanche that ended the dynastic government of the Somozas.

Hence I demand prompt justice. With nothing more to say, I greet you with all consideration.

Violeta Barrios de Chamorro

Appendix D

THE FOLLOWING BRIEF synopsis of other items censored in 1985 also reveals the nature of the Sandinista state:

PSYCHIATRIC HOSPITAL PATIENTS TO PICK COFFEE

The sending of twenty patients from the National Psychiatric Hospital to pick coffee at the farms near Managua could not be made known to the public nor to the patients' relatives, despite its having been confirmed by hospital authorities (16 January).

CONCERN OVER THE PRESIDENTIAL SASH

A question from a reader, Francisco Lezama Sinclair, about why the Nicaraguan escutcheon could not be seen on the presidential sash worn by President Ortega at his inaugural, seemed neither patriotic nor "Sandinista" to the censor (22 January).

FOOD CONFISCATED FROM THE POOR

A complaint from Boaco residents, and from travelers to that city, about the constant seizure of basic foods such as meat, cheese, cream and other products of that region, for the personal benefit of the Sandinista inspectors (19 February).

MARCIA MOJICA FIRED AT THE VICTORIA BREWERY

"The truth is that they have workers' blacklists," asserted Marcia Mojica, recently fired from the brewery. The CAUS workers union is defending her, but it couldn't defend her from the censor (22 February).

11 CIVIC LEADERS SUMMONED AND FILMED AT THE SECURITY OFFICE

The Democratic Coordinating Board leaders and the COSEP board members were summoned, without any written order, to House No. 50 of State Security at the Military Colony. The news and the names were suppressed (9 March).

FULL STOPS

People standing in long lines underscore the transportation problem in Managua and the provinces; these lines are almost identical to those that form in vain at the markets, at the neighborhood shops, at the clothing stores, and all other places where things are scarce. The photos of these lines and queues could not appear in *La Prensa* (18 March).

FOOD AND MEDICINES, TO THE TRASH DUMP

Government monopoly and hoarding of food and medicines, stored in mysterious warehouses until they rotted, caused them to be discarded in great quantities at the lake shore, in the Acahualinca trash heap where the poor of Managua desperately rushed to scavenge, seeking food and expired medicine. But the causes and the consequences, as well as the fact itself, were ignored by the censor (15 May).

THE "SACUANJOCHE," A RESTAURANT THAT DOESN'T SMELL WELL FOR THE STATE TREASURY

"El Sacuanjoche" [named after the Nicaraguan national flower] is the most luxurious and exclusive restaurant in Nicaragua, on Kilometer 8 of the Masaya Highway, available only for high government officers and friends. Its cash balance runs over 7 million. Its administrative and fiscal abnormalities would long ago have made it subject to confiscation, were it private property. It reports 5.5 million in accounts receivable and its books are not registered (as required by law) at the Register Office nor at the Tax Office (4 June).

LETTERS REVEAL MISTREATMENT OF NICARAGUANS IN BULGARIA

Nicaraguan workers suffer discrimination in Bulgaria. "You must work like a slave to pay back the equipment sent by Bulgaria to your country," a commissar told the Nicaraguans (16 June).

COST OF COFFINS, BEYOND REACH

The exorbitant cost of coffins, which the average Nicaraguan cannot afford, is censored (26 June).

DRUNK CUBAN KILLS 2 NICARAGUANS

"The Permanent Human Rights Commission (CPDH) of Nicaragua reported 104 complaints of human rights violations in the country during July 1985.

The report asserts that the Commission is particularly concerned about the death of three Nicaraguan citizens, two of whom died at the hands of a Cuban identified as one of his country's military advisers serving the Sandinista government.

Juan García Robles, age 32, resident of Nueva Guinea in the southern region of the Zelaya Department, brought the complaint against the Cuban to the CPDH.

According to García Robles, on 6 July, while at a party in the Nueva Guinea Community House, a Cuban military adviser in that region of the country began firing his .45 caliber revolver, killing two people and wounding three others.

The testimony adds that the Cuban, who appeared obviously drunk, is known in Nueva Guinea as *'El Profesor.'*

Ventura Aburto Baltodano, age 40, and Javier Rosales, 17, were two victims who perished by the shots of the foreign military man.

Mrs. Juana Vargas, Francisco Pineda, and the complainant, Juan García Robles, were wounded by the Cuban's bullets. According to his deposition, García was shot in the hip.

Two weeks after the event at the Nueva Guinea Community House, a military officer who identified himself as Danilo Brown, and said to be employed at the Ministry of the Interior, visited García Robles at home and gave him 15,000 *córdobas*.

The other wounded persons were also offered the same amount of money" (7 September).

WORRY ABOUT THE "COTTON DENGUE"

A rare disease called "cotton dengue" affects the cotton crop (13 September).

EDITORIAL

"In Ortega's statement there is a confession, too: The revolutionary process is not popular, but imposed. Were it popular, it wouldn't fear contrary opinion. It wouldn't fear criticism. If Nicaragua were free, Nicaragua would be in peace. Were Nicaragua a democracy, our revolution would be an advanced process and not this marching backwards, this suicidal return to a dictatorial system that cost us so much to destroy" (23 September).

PRT, TOO, SUPPORTS THE 13TH

Workers will not benefit from the "13th month," or Christmas bonus, because the entire amount or a percentage, in accordance with a rate table, goes to an Unemployment Fund that never renders an account. The Revolutionary Party of the Workers (PRT) denounced it, as did other parties and labor unions (26 October).

ORTEGA BUYS $3,500 EYEGLASSES

According to the Spanish news agency EFE and the *New York Times*, Daniel Ortega and his wife, Rosario Murillo, spent $3,500 in New York for modern-frame and bulletproof-glass spectacles (21 October).

ORTEGA'S EXPENSES ESTIMATED AT A MILLION AND A HALF DOLLARS

The total expenses during that trip of Ortega and his retinue, "cost the Nicaraguan people no less than a million and a half dollars, according to an estimate by Nicaraguan Communist Party leaders" (28 October).

ARRIVAL OF MEAT ATTRACTS MANY BUYERS

"Neither my children nor I have had any meat for weeks," states Anita Suárez. This and a photo of people standing in long lines were censored (11 November).

HALF-EMPTY STADIUM

The baseball season begins; the stadium is not full, so this fact is censored (30 November).

THEY ASK ABOUT RIONSITO

Readers from Ocotal ask about the popular cartoon figure Rionsito, who is often censored, as is the readers' query (16 December).

PRESS MEDIA WITH CEILINGS AND COMPENSATIONS

El Nuevo Diario denies that it is subsidized, but a document proves that it is: the document is "a detailed report of the invoices billed by the official Alfa Omega publicity agency," which is obliged to give *El Nuevo Diario* at least one million *córdobas* in paid advertisements a month. When it doesn't meet its financial obligation, it must pay *El Nuevo Diario* the balance to complete the million per month (21 December).

Appendix E

1.

THE FOLLOWING REPRESENTATIVE selections from articles or news items censored in *La Prensa* in 1986 are quoted in full:

NEED TO HALT EXODUS OF PROFESSIONALS NOTED
4 January 1986

Dr. Andrés Zúñiga, head of CONAPRO [Confederation of Professionals of Nicaragua], claimed that salary increases in Latin American countries have never solved the domestic problem because they tend to raise consumer goods prices; and if professionals have been favored, it has been to prevent an increase in the exodus of talent abroad.

In developed countries, prices of products are set in an orderly fashion, and a certain balance is kept with salary increases, so that they may bring benefits and thus be able to solve domestic problems.

Dr. Zúñiga told *La Prensa* that since 1981 CONAPRO has promoted a campaign to halt the flight of professionals, so that they might participate in the different phases of the country's reconstruction. A poster was devised, with the map of Nicaragua, and an inscription stating that the nation needs their services. But there are several factors fostering the exodus of professionals, such as the lack of security, controlled education, the lack of free enterprise, the absence of equipment or materials, and the Law on Commerce. According to Dr. Zúñiga, the government should provide greater internal confidence, to prevent the "brain drain" abroad.

The salary increase will probably retain professionals for only a little longer, because if the price of consumer goods rises, they will be motivated to leave the country.

SOCIAL CHRISTIAN YOUTHS' DEATHS DENOUNCED
5 January 1986

The death of the youth, Zacarías Martínez Coronado, 17, and the torture of Vicente Rodríquez Martínez, 18, both members of the Social Christian Party, were reported to the Permanent Human Rights Commission.

According to the report, the two youths were captured on 9 November by a Sandinista police patrol consisting of six members.

The complainants said that the captors told the boys that they were being recruited for compulsory military service, but that they were already enrolled. Instead of being enlisted in a battalion, they were taken to the El Almendro community, where they reside. On the way, they were savagely kicked and beaten with the butts of weapons, according to the relatives of the two youths. They claimed that the military left young Vicente Rodríguez on the road, believing him to be dead; but he was alive and managed to reach his residence in El Almendro. On the other hand, they said that Martínez's body was found 2 days later, in a state of decomposition, on a site known as *Valle el Chorro*, located between the county of El Carrizo and the municipality of San Isidro.

GOVERNMENT BANS CEREMONIES ON ANNIVERSARY OF *LA PRENSA* EDITOR'S ASSASSINATION
11 January 1986

Antonio Munguía Pasos, head of the Pedro Joaquín Chamorro Taxi Drivers Cooperative, reported that a few days before January 10 César Núñez, of the Interior Ministry, had visited them to warn them not to hold political ceremonies on that date.

During the visit, Núñez asked them for reports on the activities that they would hold, and whether or not they were political. Later, several representatives from the cooperative went to the Enrique Schmidt Police Station to request the pertinent permit to hold a a memorial in honor of the martyr of public freedoms. There they were told that all ceremonies were banned by the state of emergency and that on 10 January only part of the board of directors of the Taxi Drivers Cooperative could go to the cemetery to lay wreaths—but without speeches or further ceremonies. Munguía Pasos said that the only memorial that they held in front of Pedro Joaquín [Chamorro]'s grave was to sing the national anthem of Nicaragua. Then they placed the wreath which they were carrying and left.

GODOY PROTESTS ARRESTS, STATE OF EMERGENCY
23 January 1986

Virgilio Godoy, president of the Independent Liberal Party (PLI), reported today that all of the male inhabitants of the town of "El Jicote," Estelí Province, have been imprisoned by Sandinista authorities on charges of collaborating with the "counterrevolution." A total of 56 prisoners are being held in the Office of State Security prison cells in the department seat of Estelí, 140 kilometers north of Managua.

Godoy said that this information was supplied by women residing in "El Jicote," who made their report to officials of the Independent Liberal Party. "El Jicote is a small community of farmers where there now are only women and children," Godoy said.

"The only successful program of the Sandinista Government is the construction of prisons, and this proves it," the leader of the Liberal Party in Nicaragua asserted.

Godoy told a group of journalists who had visited him in his office on October 15, 1985, when new restrictions on the Nicaraguan people's freedoms were announced, that the Sandinista Revolution had "initiated a deterioration" in its world image.

The PLI president said that recent statements by the foreign minister of Argentina, Dante Caputo, that the persistence of a pro-Soviet ideology is not compatible with peace in Central America demonstrates the isolation of Nicaragua's government. "These were very strong statements," Godoy said.

He also said, "The Socialist International involved itself in Nicaragua as if it were a major project, but it has become disillusioned and is now pressuring the Sandinista Government to find an appropriate way out."

Godoy rejected assertions that a new Constitution is a sign of democracy in Nicaragua, as claimed by the government.

"It is important to know whether or not that Constitution is going to be applied. We have never been without a Constitution. The *Statute of Human Rights* and *Guarantees of the Nicaraguan People*, which became effective with the victory of the revolution, says a lot of nice things but none of them has been carried out," the PLI leader said.

"What remains unknown is whether or not the Constitution will be applied in Nicaragua," he added.

The PLI, along with the Socialist Party, has withdrawn from the discussion of the Constitution, which is taking place in the National Assembly. The leaders of both parties allege that because of the state-of-emergency restrictions there are insufficient civil guarantees to produce a democratic discussion of the new Constitution. Godoy said that about 10 percent of the country's current population has fled from Nicaragua because of political and economic instability.

"School enrollment has dropped 36 percent this year, since out of the 1.1 million students enrolled in 1984, the Ministry of Education expects an enrollment of only 700,000 students in 1986," Godoy said.

CONSUMERS FIND LARD INEDIBLE, USE IT TO MAKE CANDLES

28 January 1986

Boaco—A large number of Nicaraguans became ill after eating food fried in the lard being sold at supply centers. There has been such a rejection of this product that even the poorest families are refusing to use it.

On this subject, one food store owner said: "This product is so bad and since it is real tallow, I decided to make candles out of it, since these too are in short supply, and I've had good results. Now, they're calling them lard candles instead of tallow candles."

POLITICAL PARTIES NOT IN NATIONAL ASSEMBLY RESTRICTED

30 January 1986

Comandante Doris Tijerino, national chief of the Sandinista Police, unexpectedly issued a communiqué in which she states that the emergency law now in force had not affected the activities of political parties, at a time when the Sandinista National Liberation Front (FSLN) Government was announcing a continental conference of political parties in Managua.

According to the regulations announced by Comandante Tijerino, it now appears that the political parties represented in the National Assembly have the right to organize public events, if they request police permission at least one week in advance.

Those parties that are not represented in the assembly because they refused to participate in the elections of November 1984 are not entitled to these new privileges. According to Comandante Tijerino, only those parties which participated with the FSLN in the 1984 electoral campaign have a right to hold meetings and to disseminate their political programs.

In the meantime, the deputy coordinator of the FSLN announced this week that a conference will be held in Managua for political parties of the American continent, which will be attended by about 112 delegates, according to government estimates.

The FSLN has also sent invitations to the leaders of the three most important international political groups: the Christian Democratic, Socialist, and Liberal groups.

Andrés Zaldívar, head of the Christian Democratic group, has declined the invitation. According to official sources, the Socialist International will send a delegation headed by Carlos Andrés Peréz and a Socialist parliamentarian from Italy.

OBANDO DENOUNCES HUMAN RIGHTS VIOLATIONS
24 April 1986

Cardinal Miguel Obando y Bravo declared on Sunday that the Nicaraguan Catholic Church condemns human rights violations no matter who commits them, and he expressed his disapproval of the recent events in Somotillo where six civilians were killed during an ambush.

During his homily at the Sunday religious service in the parish of Santo Domingo, Obando said that the Catholic Church of Nicaragua does not now have many ways to make its voice heard; however, he emphasized that the Church will always assume the responsibility of denouncing violations of human rights, without regard for ideologies.

At the same time, the Cardinal said that he had received a petition from several priests in the department of Granada requesting the prayers of the faithful, because the former had received summonses to report to the offices of state security.

The Cardinal, who at the end of his homily received the unanimous applause of the parishioners present, said, "This is the only thing we have left [the microphone] to make the voice of the Church heard."

"We do not have a radio station, Sunday newsletter, or any other way to make our voice heard," his Eminence added.

With regard to the ambush near Somotillo, where an internationalist of Swiss nationality was killed, the Cardinal said that an impartial investigation of the facts was required.

2.

In addition, the following is a synopsis of other representative examples of Sandinista censorship in 1986:

TRAVERSING NICARAGUA

The El Carmen village, as a community, acquired a transport vehicle and gave it to the municipal authorities who in turn sold it or gave it away for "other uses." (3 January)

TWO JOBS TO SURVIVE

In Tanzania, in remote Africa, professionals and bureaucrats must resort to two jobs and a "shamba" or vegetable garden to survive. According to the censor, this was a veiled attack against the Sandinista Revolution and the Sandinista New Man. (5 January)

EDITORIAL

"Political fraud has been an essential weapon in the Sandinista arsenal since the organization was founded in 1961. (Each year they move the date backwards; perhaps they will discover that Sandino or Rubén Dario [who died in 1933 and 1916 respectively] founded it.) Carlos Fonseca, one of the founders and its chief theorist till his death in the '70s, understood that unadulterated Marxism-Leninism would hinder and probably prevent any effort to spark the national insurrection needed to overthrow Somoza. Hence, the incipient guerrilla front appropriated the image of Sandino, a national hero who fought the U.S. Marines three decades earlier." (5 January)

RUBÉN DARIO'S FULL-DRESS SUIT HAS DISAPPEARED

It was enough to submit the caption "Rubén Dario's full-dress suit has disappeared," for the censor to reject both the caption and the article. (7 January)

EDITORIAL

"*La Prensa*, with all its good will and in its desire to see no more Nicaraguan blood shed, asks President Reagan to accept the proposal of the thirty-one congressmen and delay his request for aid to the armed Nicaraguan opposition, and we also ask *Contadora* to achieve in the next forty-five days what it has been eagerly seeking during the past three years, that is, a level of high and candid negotiations among the five Central American nations. Democracy in Nicaragua would bring immediate peace to the region, and with it would come progress and development." (11 February)

WELCOME, YOUR EXCELLENCY

"National dialogue, is the cry of the people all over the country. Dialogue and peace, repeat our beloved shepherds the Catholic bishops headed by His Eminence Cardinal Obando y Bravo—all who have endured indecent slanders in their indefatigable labors preaching the gospel of Love." (15 January)

TWO *LA PRENSA* JOURNALISTS IN JAIL

La Prensa journalists Alejandro Cordonero and Enrique García were arrested by the State Security. The news could not be published. (18 January)

PATIENT SENT HOME UNCONSCIOUS BECAUSE HE HAD BEEN "DISCHARGED"

A patient still unconscious under anesthesia was expelled from the Lenín Fonseca Hospital, "discharged" in true military fashion, by two policemen. (20 January)

THE NATIONAL DIALOGUE, THE ONLY ROAD TO PEACE

Because the words "Dialogue" and "Peace" appeared in our headline "The National Dialogue, the Only Road to Peace," it was censored on 24 January.

RECOGNITION OF AN HONORABLE OCCUPATION

When salaries were readjusted in an attempt to compensate for inflation, *La Prensa* pleaded for social justice, asking that the readjustment should also include housemaids. (26 January)

A RIGHT JAB FROM ALEXIS KO'D COSTELLO!

The allusion to world-boxing champion, Alexis Argüello, was censored on 10 February.

LITTLE PROGRESS IN THE RAILROAD

The Railroad, called in jest "rail-turtle" in the Somoza era, has not improved under the Sandinistas; this was censored 12 February.

EDITORIAL

"We insist that it isn't enough to paint white doves everywhere in order to advance towards peace. After the fiery speeches of the southpaw-left and its panegyrists, many of them old fossils, quite senile, who repeat from the rostrum the same old words...these gentlemen should know that their speeches will not save the Nicaraguan people from a larger conflict." (13 February)

LIBERTY CHARTER FIRST

"The dead, the destruction, the tears, and the pain come from the Nicaraguan people, to whom the Sandinista leadership has a much greater moral obligation than President Reagan, the presidents of Contadora, and the Support Group, who may patiently take their time in solving the problems of the world so long as their own people's blood is not being shed." (15 February)

THE CONTRADICTIONS OF A MEETING AND THE FSLN

"The Nicaraguan people do not realize how much they pay for the events promoted by the Sandinista Front (FSLN) political party. They do not realize the amounts on bills for many rooms at the Intercontinental Hotel, for the use of dozens of luxurious cars, the airline tickets, the courtesies, the fuel, the receptions, the snacks and tidbits, the dinners, the drinks; the misused man-hours of policemen, of guardsmen, of escorts, of aides-de-camp; the broadcasts on the two official TV channels, the closing of inaugural speeches; and the many other miscellaneous expenses." (17 February)

COCKROACH CAUSES FIRING OF TWO WORKERS

A cockroach caused the firing of Luisa Tiffer and Alba Siles, both of whom worked in the kitchen at the Match Factory. They found a cockroach in the dough and complained; they were told to say nothing about it and simply to to "strain the dough." They complained, and were fired. (20 February)

LA PRENSA IS OF THE PEOPLE, WHO WON'T ALLOW THE NEWSPAPER OF THE NICARAGUAN PEOPLE TO BE KILLED

On 26 February, a headline from an interview with Francisco Alvarado, last survivor of the founding *La Prensa* workers of 1926, which said,

"*La Prensa* is of the people, who won't allow the Newspaper of the Nicaraguan people to be killed," was censored as was Circulation Manager Rafael Bonilla's comments on Somocista and Sandinista censorship.

Appendix F

Talking with Pablo Antonio

WHILE COMMEMORATING *La Prensa*'s 60th anniversary, 2 March 1986, *La Prensa Literaria* interviewed Pablo Antonio Cuadra, *La Prensa*'s director and the creator of its literary supplement. The questions related to the past and future of Nicaraguan journalism and culture.

The censor, however, showed no respect, neither for the person nor his work—Pablo Antonio is a renowned Nicaraguan poet—nor for the anniversary or the institution and hence suppressed a good part of the interview given on 1 March 1986, on National Journalism Day.

We have included the complete interview.

Q. Sixty years, poet, thirty-six of which are yours...

A. Maybe a few more, because of my earlier links with those *Lunes de la "Prensa"* [Mondays of *"La Prensa"*] and the *Semana* [Week] magazine. But for a full history, perhaps it would be useful to give a synthesis of *La Prensa*'s beginning and its stages, which Mario Cajina is now narrating in volumes and with panoramic views of each period. In its first stage, *La Prensa* was a political party newspaper, something quite common in Hispanic America; indeed, the first stage of the Sandinista regime has been to create party newspapers, too.

So, in 1948 *La Prensa* was a party newspaper, Conservative to boot, and through it was waged the first generational battle around Sandino, the authentic General Sandino and not the fake one they have created. A great poet, Salomón de la Selva in Buitrago Díaz's *La Tribuna*, and another poet and great journalist, Ortega Díaz, editor of *La Prensa*, had already fought against American intervention when the guerilla fighter was alive. In this we see *La Prensa*'s destiny, of being a patriotic, Nicaraguan voice. Afterwards, in the '40s, Pedro Joaquín returned from Mexico and began with his father to build a modern newspaper, different from the political-party journalism. He made it an objective, informative daily: editorially he waged a battle for democracy against the dictatorship, and he became a public prosecutor on behalf of his country, while simultaneously developing the news reporting and stimulating a free forum for debate and collaboration. Thus began the struggle that continues today.

In 1952, with resistance on my part because of my love for the countryside, Don Pedro, quite ill, called on me to become coeditor-in-chief. I assumed that post in 1953, and so began my life inside *La Prensa*, with Pedro Joaquín at my side. He was, as the people later anointed him, "the incorruptible Pedro." In 1954, a few months after I became coeditor, Pedro took part in the April rebellion and was captured. Having two editors begins to have meaning, for I remained at *La Prensa* confronting the Somocista beasts that wanted to exterminate us.

Q. And abruptly, censorship falls on *La Prensa*...

A. Even including the prohibition, so typically Latin American, that censorship be kept secret. We are forced to conceal the very crimes the regime commits against us; it is a pharisaism typical of our dictatorships. The censor wished to make it an inane daily paper, with the deliberate presidential will of purposely killing it. This is, of course, especially painful now that we suffer the same, and I remember also the time when Somocista censorship was so severe that there was nothing to fill the blanks with, and so I inserted a photo of Ava Gardner, the beautiful movie star then in fashion. That evening, the phone rang, and the censor asked: "What does Ava Gardner mean on the front page, and without a photo caption?" —Our answer: "It means censorship. Ava fills the blanks you made." This became public, and once it transpired that we were being gagged and manacled, our newsboys were quickly out into the streets shouting, with unrestrained Nicaraguan wit, *"La Prensa*, with Ava Gardner!" as a way of announcing that we had been censored. If Ava Gardner, close friend of Hemingway, knew about it...perhaps today we could fill the blanks with Jane Fonda, but this time not even that is allowed!

Q. 1954...no sooner was it lifted, censorship was imposed again...

A. In 1956, two years later, after the assassination of Somoza. All of us at *La Prensa* were jailed: we were among two thousand opponents made captive in Managua. Somoza's sons wanted at all costs to implicate Pedro Joaquín as an accomplice or participant in the execution of their father. They failed, because the person they had tortured into bearing false witness backed off at the trial before the Military Court, and with extraordinary fortitude told them: "What I declared under torture is false: I did it because they were killing me and I was out of my mind." And he ruined their entire plan in front of the Nicaraguan journalists, the television cameras, and the international correspondents. That man is Horacio Ruiz, our best editor and a symbol for us. Deplorably, today he has again been a victim of the violence against freedom.

Q. You, poet, you had to "managerialize yourself" between jail and jail...

A. Yes. But parallel to the newspaper, I strove to crystallize culture, which is my vocation; thus, the Sunday Supplement became *La Prensa Literaria*, whose pages collect and preserve modern Nicaraguan culture. A friend has told me that it "creates culture for all Nicaraguans." I only work and fulfill myself trying to follow the spirit's star as a guide. The national sensibility should be nurtured with readings that are instructively renascent and that reinforce the country's civic values which the intellectual, by his very mission, cannot ignore. Afterwards, in 1959, Pedro Joaquín landed as an insurgent from exile in the Olama and Los Mollejones expedition against the two sons of Somoza.

Q. And back to censorship...

A. And back to censorship! That is how we live: Between censorship and freedom. The grave problem is that civilization starts when man no longer has to fear for his right to life, and political civilization starts when freedom of speech is an accepted fact. As long as we must concern ourselves with the fight for our security and our opinion, our political system will never arrive at what is called civilization. Humanism begins with liberty.

Q. In those intermittent throes of death, what became of the modern journalism proposed at the beginning?

A. Technically, we had become efficient; and we kept alive our independent spirit at all cost. Thus when they gave us in Guatemala the award as the best newspaper of Central America, I spoke of "the idea of *La Prensa*: Socratic journalism." For its principles and reflections, I drew on my various talks with Pedro Joaquín: with the arrival of radio and television and with the speed that the electronic media provides the news, the journalism we were creating could no longer be influenced by American journalism: the "latest hot news" and "the latest extra." That dynamic was on the way out, superceded by audiovisual "live reporting" and "up to the minute news."

Because of this radical change in world journalism—in the new media, printed matter came "cold" and slow. We then thought of a normative journalism—that the news could serve as a basis for a philosophical and anthropological exposition showing from top to bottom, life, politics, and culture. That is what I called "Socratic journalism," seeking the essence of things through reporting, dialogue, and even irony, which is what Socrates did in the Agora and on the streets of turbulent Greece. The philosopher turned the news into a road to truth, through questioning and reasoning; in short: through dialogue. We also endeavored to create a culture drawn from our own roots—from the Nicaraguan people themselves. Thus we pushed for a journalistic revolution: knowing our essential reality, we wouldn't have to improvise. From partisan politics and news journalism, our paper aimed at crystallizing the reality of everyday life—the anguished philosophy of the ephemeral, keeping the human condition always in sight.

Q. "Socratic journalism" requires freedom...

A. Like all superior works of man do. As an ideal, Socratic journalism is the opposite of the journalism from above, directive and arrogant. One of our most popular sections was *La Voz del Pueblo* [The Voice of the People]; it sprouted from below, from the root of the people's scream, and as we saw what the people thought of each event and of each thing, we naturally refused to close the door to reality, contrary to those ideological models that predominate so much today, with their totalitarianism. I believe that the people never had so open an access to a newspaper as they did in *La Prensa* during its last ten years before Pedro Joaquín died. There we earned, born from the very entrails of the public, the historical definition of "The Newspaper of the Nicaraguan People." Our fundamental fight has been for freedom of speech and for creative criticism; all imperfections can be corrected if there is criticism to modify them. But today the totalitarian paradigmatic schemes and models wish to subjugate our realities and hopes, silencing them to impose abstractions over facts, scandalizing those of us who gave ourselves wholeheartedly to a Nicaraguan Revolution. But a revolution without freedom and without criticism turns into its own counterrevolution.

Q. Was it, again, the return to barbarism?

A. The values of *La Prensa* were again threatened by a return to periodic barbarism. Confronting the dictatorial, dynastic power, *La Prensa*—banner of liberty—was then called "The Paper Republic." Why did we call it this?

Because the violence and the censorship converted *La Prensa* into the last bulwark of republicanism and of democratic practices.

Despite all the dictatorial obstacles, our paper became the refuge of free men and women with free thoughts and the tribune, frequently silenced, of pluralistic and democratic ideals. *La Prensa* is all the people who suffer! How many suffered jail, persecution, vexations, ill will, only because they published their opinions in *La Prensa*! It is a history of adding up and carrying forward. Afterwards, the tragedy and heroism of its Martyred-Editor, Pedro Joaquín Chamorro, was followed months later by the bombing and the destruction of the paper as a farewell from the dictator seeking its final extinction: these are the two sacrifices, the two immolations, the two sparks that set on fire the insurrectionary explosion against the dynasty. And now...a revolution that began by the death of a free journalist and continued by the destruction of a free newspaper, plunges, no sooner than it triumphs, into the worst betrayal ever suffered in Nicaragua. And what is the reason? To impose, at the price of liberty, a neototalitarianism of Marxist cut, unnecessary and aberrant in our Nicaraguan Revolution because here, as opposed to Cuba, there was no void to fill. Not here! Here Pedro Joaquín, whose blood toppled the Somozas, had already formed—and at what cost, and how much sacrifice but also with so much popular support—a national unity, a plurality of popular opinions fusing both the left and right to the center of Nicaraguan reality. In the great victory of his death, when the entire country rose in rebellion, we see how he was creating a national ideology, a nationalistic fusion of all tendencies—how he was creating the ideas for an authentic Nicaraguan Revolution, for freedom and justice, pluralistic and republican, democratic and nationalist.

Let this be clear: On adopting the ideas of Marxism-Leninism, *Sandinismo* is not—I repeat—filling a void like they did in Cuba. Here we had a system of ideas intrinsic to our Revolution, gained with sacrifices, victims, martyrs, and with an independent newspaper supported by the people.

But no. Censorship once more paralyzed our aspirations, pressing its gauntlet to our throat to keep us from writing and speaking; hence we return to obscurantism.

Q. You have said that when *La Prensa* had freedom it raised the journalistic and cultural levels of Central America; and when it didn't have it, it has fought to restore the nexus between culture and freedom...

A. Within that fight, in both instances the case of *La Prensa* is unique. It hasn't been precisely a model of the fourth estate as the press in general is called, but perhaps a unique case of fourth impotence, because our paper, despite its long history of confrontation with abusive national and foreign powers, and despite the sacrifice of its murdered editor and the backing of the people who always support it (which is crucial because it means that freedom of speech is the spontaneous yearning of the people)—despite all this—*La Prensa* has always been forced to submit to censorship, under different pretexts and regimes but with all too similar purposes and analogous methods...

Q. It is because freedom, poet, has so many enemies!

A. Besides enemies, I would add opportunistic and superficial minds that easily forget that man *is,* only if he *is free.* His dignity is built on that foundation: Freedom...But let us imagine the fragile splendor of freedom and let us think that freedom of speech is not really a goal —it is a starting point, the initial impulse for the practice and the fulfillment of being wholly human. That humanism is the vocation of this newspaper. That is why it fights, that is why it will die, if it must, to preserve the legacy of what is fundamental and true in Nicaraguan history.

Appendix G

LETTER OF VIOLETA BARRIOS DE CHAMORRO SENT TO DANIEL ORTEGA, 7 JUNE 1988

Señor Presidente de la República
Comandante Daniel Ortega
Managua, 7 June 1988

I bring before you my strongest protest against the injurious campaign mounted against me by the Sandinista Television System—the informative medium of your state Party, which has reached vulgar and dangerous extremes never before seen in our nation.

The most recent campaign of this propagandistic arm of Sandinismo, also reproduced by your Party newspapers, *Barricada* and *El Nuevo Diario*, publicly shows the sacred remains of my husband, ridden with gunshot wounds, next to photographs or videos of myself, taken out of context, and which show me as appearing grateful for my husband's assassination.

Señor Ortega: When you came to my house [on 19 September 1987], pressured by the circumstances of the moment, to offer me a shady agreement for the reopening of *La Prensa*, not only did I refuse it but with Don Rodrigo Madrigal Nieto, the foreign minister of Costa Rica, as a witness, I clearly told you that *La Prensa* would either be published without censorship or it would not be published at all. In addition, I refused to accept as a form of indirect pressure "the responsible exercise of journalism"—

a phrase that your negotiators wanted to impose on me in order to insinuate that a prearranged agreement had been devised for the reopening of *La Prensa*.

You know very well that *La Prensa*, in its new stage of life, survived a brutal closing for fourteen months, arbitrarily imposed by your government, and you also know that it will continue to develop an undeviating journalism in behalf of the people's interests, without ignoring the many vices that distinguish your government's actions.

If you, in spite of this, permitted *La Prensa*'s reopening as a result of Esquipulas II [signed in Guatemala 7 August 1987] and not from any good will, then you should know that you will have to tolerate responsible criticism of your actions and those of your functionaries—as is the case in every democratic country—a state of democracy that was the goal of the Guatemala accord that you signed guaranteeing compliance with its articles.

But the vacillations and duplicities of your government in regard to this compliance compel us to speak the truth: your government has demonstrated that it does not want to honor the accord you signed, and it is my obligation and *La Prensa*'s to reveal this to both the Nicaraguan people and the civilized world.

I would also point out that it has been your government, and not *La Prensa*, that negotiated with the Nicaraguan Resistance in spite of having frequently insisted that it would never do so. And since among the delegates of the Nicaraguan Resistance, Comandante Enrique Bermúdez, former colonel in the National Guard, has also arrived to negotiate—it is exclusively your government that has accepted him as a legitimate interlocutor.

If these negotiations are not favorable for the political interests of your state Party, the blame will belong to your government—not to me nor *La Prensa*, which limits itself only to tell the truth. In this case, the truth, whether you like it or not, consists in showing that your government, in addition to ruining the country, has dedicated itself to the liquidation of all rebellion, without correspondingly restoring any of the basic human rights of the Nicaraguan people.

Your government, besieged by disaster and inefficiency and by the incompetence of its functionaries, is obligated to comply with Esquipulas II, and you, your functionaries, and state employees all know it.

All Nicaragua knows that you and your government have ruined the country and that, consequently, compliance with the peace accord can no longer be delayed—an accord that requires the restoration of the Nicaraguan people's human rights and their liberties, long confiscated.

Even the Soviet Union and its satellites have grown weary of this tremendous disaster, and it is widely known that they are no longer committed to your political and military survival.

In regard to all the above, neither *La Prensa* nor myself is to blame, much less the memory of my husband Pedro Joaquín Chamorro—a memory that should be, above all, sacred to you, the Sandinistas, beneficiaries of his death.

The exhibition of my husband's body—destroyed by assassin bullets whose origin I am uncertain of even today—transmitted and publicized through the infamous media of your state Party, together with images of myself suggesting my satisfaction with his death, constitutes a cowardly and repugnant act that can only be explained by the miserable morality that distinguishes your government.

It is one thing to attempt to hide from the people and your own Party members the weakness of you and your government—a weakness that might even lead to your compliance with Esquipulas II—forced by the terrible reality that we are living through today. But it is something else to attempt to camouflage this reality, exposing through the state media the desecrated body of my husband—a man declared "Martyr of Public Liberties" by your own law—and insulting and slandering his widow, who as both a widow and woman deserves a minimum degree of respect. In any country this would be called villainy, infamy, and ignominy: all characteristics of your immoral government—a government that I helped and supported when I was carried away with the strong emotions that characterize a woman, actions which I repent and abhor as I do my sins.

As a Nicaraguan I work for peace. As a woman I unite myself with the widows and mothers of Nicaragua who suffer so much because of your government. And as director of *La Prensa*, I promise you that I will continue denouncing and combating the acts of your government, until you and your government silence me with the brutal club or the assassin's bullet.

Index

Index

Aguilar, Eloy O., 86
Aguirre, Danilo, 19, 25-29
Allende, Salvador, 30-31
Alonso, Máximo, 40, 111
Amador, Guillermo, 140
Ampié Calero, Carlos, 140
Anderson, Jack, 53
Andrés Pérez, Carlos, 67, 90
Arce, Bayardo, 9, 19, 25, 28, 43, 140, 143
Argentina, 52
Argüello, Alexis, 23, 55
Argüello, Leonardo, 3
Argüello Hurtado, Roberto, 72-73
Arias Caldera, Fr., 80
Armas, Julio, 138
Atlantic Coast, 40, 51
Avance, 19

Barricada, 15, 18, 30, 37, 52-54, 58, 79-82, 101-102, 109, 112, 127-129, 143
Barrios de Chamorro, Violeta, 3-4, 26-28, 51, 56, 60, 63, 67-74, 78, 131, 135—142
Belli, Enrique, 1
Belli, Gioconda, 7
Belli, Humberto, 40
Belli, Pedro, 1
Bermudez, General, 74
Blandón, Nelba Cecilia, 21, 52, 54, 61-62, 81, 86, 93, 105-108, 129, 137
Bluefields, 29-30
Bolaños family, 107
Bonilla, Rafael, 29
Borge, Tomás, 9, 17, 33, 43-45, 51, 57, 68-72, 87-89, 94, 105, 126, 142
Brenes Jarquín, Carlos, 2
Bulgaria, 81, 87

Calvo Arrieta, Salomón, 22
Carazo Odio, Rodrigo, 67
Cardenal, Ernesto, 7, 17, 37

Cardenal, Roberto, 40, 77, 79, 94
Cardenal de Chamorro, Margarita, 26
Carter, Jimmy, 89
Carter administration, 10
Casa 50, 40, 138
Castillo, Edgard, 29
Castillo, José María, 10
Castillo Martínez, Ernesto, 11, 70, 71
Castillo Osejo, José, 142
Castro, Fidel, 4, 26, 68, 126
Castro Barahone, Lucrecia del Carmen, 66
Catholic Church, 22, 77-85
Census and Statistics National Institute (INEC), 35
Center for Promotion and Development (CEPAD), 100
Center of Nicaraguan Workers (CTN), 22, 78
Centroamericano, El, 15
Cerna, Lenín, 57, 74-75, 102, 108
César, Alfredo, 90
Chamorro, Carlos Fernando, 57
Chamorro, Claudia, 73
Chamorro, Diego Manuel, 1
Chamorro, Emiliano, 1
Chamorro, Fruto, 1
Chamorro, Jaime, 77, 94-95, 131-133, 141
Chamorro, Negro, 44
Chamorro, Pedro Joaquín, 1
Chamorro, Xavier, 11, 19, 24-29, 73, 129
Chamorro Barrios, Pedro Joaquín, 25-26, 44, 60, 72-73, 94-95 103-105
Chamorro Cardenal, Pedro Joaquín, 3-13, 24-26, 29, 39, 43, 60-62, 133, 137, 140
  murder of, 65-75
Chamorro Zelaya, Pedro Joaquín, 1-2
Chile, 30-31, 109

Chontales, 82
Christian Brothers, 90
CIA, 22, 28-31, 51-52, 87, 101, 108-109, 125, 132-133
Committee for Democracy, 104
Communist party, 19, 109, 143
¿Cómo Vamos?, 23
Confederation for Labor Unity (CUS), 22
Conservative Party, 1, 139
Constitution of 1987, 137
Contadora process, 131-132
Contras, 22, 52, 73, 100-101, 108, 110, 125, 129-133, 141
COPROSA, 82
Cordonero, Alejandro, 111, 138
Cordón Morice, Raúl, 137
Córdova Rivas, Rafael, 30, 62
Corea, Juan Carlos, 142
COSEP, 23, 32
Costa Rica, 10, 22, 36, 43, 72-73, 94, 98, 138
Council of State, 27, 30, 32
Cruz, Arturo, 30, 91-92
Cuadernos de Periodismo, 86
Cuadra, Pablo Antonio, 3, 7, 24, 29, 44, 58, 61, 127, 141
Cuba, 4, 25-26, 29-32, 37, 68, 87, 102, 106, 112

Daily Gleaner, 30-31
Dávila, Orlando Ney, 90
Debayle, Salvadora, 2
De Cara al Pueblo (TV show), 100
Decree No. 8: Abolishment of Repressive Laws, 16
Decree No. 10: Law of National Emergency, 17
Decree No. 48: General Provisional Law on Communications Media, 16-17, 132
Decree No. 102, 35
Decree No. 128: State of National Emergency, 111
Decree No. 417: Protection Law, 93
Decree No. 511: Law to Regulate Information about National Security, 16-17, 20, 30, 34-35
Decree No. 512: Law to Regulate Economic Information, 16-17, 20, 35
Decree No. 566, 60
Decree No. 708, 16
Decree No. 812: Economic and Social Emergency Law, 35
Decree No. 888, 35
Decree No. 996, 54
Decree of Suspension of Rights and Guarantees of the Nicaragua People (1985), 105
Defense Committees, 51
Democratic Conservative Party, 23
Democratic Coordinating Board (CDN), 92, 139
Democratic Union for Liberation (UDEL), 68
D'Escoto, Miguel, 34-36, 80, 83-85
Diario de un Preso (A Prisoner's Diary), 4
Diaz, Etelvína, 140
Díaz, Mario, 23

East Germany, 87, 109
Echegoyen, Auxiliadora, 40
Election of 1984, 91-93
El Salvador, 53, 102, 138
En Marcha, 23
Enríquez, Manuel Espinoza, 30
Episcopal Conference of Nicaraguan Bishops, 82-84
Escobar, Octavio, 29
Espinoza Enríquez, Manuel, 18
Estación Equis, 19
Estirpe Sangrienta: Los Somoza (The Bloody Lineage: The Somozas), 4-5, 13

Fernández, Ana Corina, 86
Ferrety, Walter, 57
Flores, Cruz, 139
Fonseca Amador, Carlos, 34, 67
Free Democratic Party (West Germany), 15
Friedrich Naumann Foundation, 15
FSLN. *See* Sandinistas
Fundamental Statute of the Republic, 16

Gaceta, La, 17
Gadea, Fabio, 18, 20, 39, 103
García, Enrique, 111, 138
Godoy, Virgilio, 100
González, José Esteban, 39, 43-44
Granada, 82
Granados Ordóñez, Humberto de la Concepción, 75
Guatemala, 127, 138
Guatemala peace plan, 141-142
Guerrero, Lorenzo, 8
Guillén, Adriana, 43-44

Haig, Alexander, 60
Hernández, Lino, 23, 139
Holmann, Anita, 26-28
Holmann, Carlos, 26-28, 77, 94
Honduras, 138

Iglesia, 22, 82
Independent Liberal Party (PLI), 23, 78, 91-92, 100
Inter-American Press Association (IAPA), 15-16, 128, 142

Jamaica, 30
Jinotega, 78
Jiron, Manuel, 20
John Paul II, 80-81
Juárez, Lolo, 78
Junta, Sandinista, 20, 27, 30, 33
Juventud Sandinista, 57, 143

Kirkpatrick, Jeane, 141
Kissinger, Henry, 77

La Prensa on Air (radio program), 105
Larios, Bernardino, 90
Law of Elucidations and Rectifications, 12
León, 15
León Carranza, Róger, 138
Leplant, Fr., 91
Liberal party, 1
López, Federico, 37, 40
Loza, Oscar, 137

Madrigal Nieto, Rodrigo, 138

Mairena, Victor, 140
Managua, 2
Manley, Michael, 30
Maradiaga, Edwin, 90
Marines, U.S., 8
Martín Morales, Edgar, 57
Marxism-Leninism, 8-11, 33, 37, 68, 112, 144
Media Office, 33-36
Medina, Víctor, 40
Mejía Godoy, Carlos, 7, 37
Mercado Madrigal, Sergio, 57
Mercurio, El, 30-31, 134
Mexico, 10, 36, 86
Ministry of Industry, 55
Ministry of Interior, 43
Miskito Indians, 29-30, 40, 43
Moncada, José Maria, 1
Montalván, Oscar, 19, 39
Montenegro, Rosa Argentina, 10
Montoneros, 31
Mora Sánchez, Luis, 22, 78, 90, 111
Murillo, Andrés, 3
Murillo, Rosario, 7-9, 24, 37

Nación, La (Costa Rica), 73
Najlis, Michelle, 33
Nandaime, 143
National Autonomous University of Nicaragua (UNAN), 31, 86
National Endowment for Democracy (NED), 108-109
National Guard, 2, 8-9, 12, 52, 73
National Literacy Campaign, 7
National Literacy Plan, 6
National Statistics System, 35
Navas Sálomon, Sergio, 140
Nicaraguan Bar Association, 91, 110, 139
Nicaraguan Democratic Movement (MDN), 20, 30, 39-40
Nicaraguan Institute of Tourism, 99
Noticiero Sandinista (TV program), 80
Novedades, 15, 18, 65
Nuevo Diario, El, 11, 19, 29-30, 37, 52-54, 58, 73, 79-80, 101-102, 109, 127-129, 140, 143

Núñez, Carlos, 28
Núñez, René, 128

Obando y Bravo, Miguel, 10, 20-22, 36, 55, 79-80, 83-85, 127
Ordóñez, Víctor Manuel, 68-69
Organization of American States, 10, 133
Orozco, Mauricio, 39
Ortega, Guillermo, 29
Ortega, Humberto, 28, 40, 60
Ortega, Daniel, 9, 18, 24, 33, 37, 60, 82, 105-107, 110, 132-143
Ortega Díaz, Adolfo, 1
Ortega Rayo, Jorge, 111

Palestine Liberation Organization, 31, 53
Pallais, Marcel, 69
Pallais Debayle, Luis, 65
Panama, 36
Paraguay, 109
Paso a Paso, 23
Pastora, Edén, 11, 34, 55, 90
Patriotic Literacy Plan, 6
Peña, Silvio, 65-66, 69-71
Penal Code of 1974, 12
Periódico, El (Mexico), 36
Permanent Human Rights Commission (CPDH), 23, 34, 139
Picasso, Claudio, 57
Plasma Pheresis Centro Americana, 66
Poland, 38
Poliedro, 92
Prensa, La
  assault on (1982), 42-63
  beginning of the end, 107-126
  in early Sandinista period, 15-32
  founding of, 1-2
  goals of, 7-8
  institutionalized repression of, 33-41
  recently, 127-147
  under Somoza regime, 2-13

  tourists and travelers to, 99-106
Prensa Gráfica, La, 18
Prensa Literaria, La, 7, 37, 127
Press Law of 1953, 12
Press Law of 1967, 12
PRI (Mexico), 86
Prisma, 23, 111
Pueblo, El, 19

Radio 590, 21
Radio Amor, 20
Radio Católica, 20-24, 83, 129, 140, 144
Radio Corporación, 10, 20, 23-24, 105, 142-144
Radio Fabuloso Siete, 10, 21
Radio Futura, 10
Radio Impacto, 22
Radio Mil, 21, 39
Radio Mi Preferida, 10, 20
Radio Mundial, 10, 20-23
Radio Nacional, 19
Radio San Cristóbal, 21
Radio Sandino, 19, 60
Radio Tiempo, 20
Rama Indians, 40
Ramírez, Carlos, 29
Ramírez, Sergio, 7-9, 37, 59, 68, 92
Ramírez, William, 9
Ramírez Artola, José, 111
Ramos, Pedro, 66
Reagan administration, 60, 110, 132-133
Reyes, Vilma Auxiliadora, 20
Rionsito (comic strip), 106
Rivas, Gabry, 1
Robelo, Alfonso, 20, 27, 30
Robleto Palma, José Antonio, 57
Ruiz, Horacio, 2-4, 25, 29, 57-58, 101

Saborío, Alberto, 139
Sacasa, Juan Bautista, 2
Sacasa-Raskowsky and Company, 18
Saimsa, 107
Salazar, Jorge, 32, 43
Sánchez, Abelardo, 40

Sandinismo, 25, 51, 62, 86, 112, 125-126, 144, 147
Sandinista Front of National Liberation. *See* Sandinistas
Sandinista revolution, 11, 40
  future of, 127-145
Sandinistas
  beginnings of, 8-13
  coming to power, 65-67
  early years in power, 15-32
  international support for, 99-106
  repression by, 33-41
Sandinista Television System (SSTV), 18
Sandinista Union, 25
Sandino, Augusto César, 2, 8, 67
Sandino, Sócrates, 2
Sapoá agreement, 141
Schick, René, 8
72-hour Document, 31-32
Sevilla, Nicolasa, 5
Social Christian Party, 104, 136
Solidaridad, 22, 23
Solidarity (Poland), 38
Somocismo, 12, 18, 33, 51, 62, 125-126
Somoza Debayle, Anastasio, 4, 8-13, 19, 24, 52, 65, 68, 75
Somoza Debayle, Luis, 4-8, 12
Somoza García, Anastasio, 2-4, 12-13, 92
Somoza Portocarrero, Anastasio, 67-69, 74
Soviet Union, 25, 31, 53, 87, 107, 128, 143
Spain, 127
Stalinization, 112
Standard Fruit Company, 33
Statute on the Rights and Guarantees of the Nicaraguan People, 16
Suárez, Fidelina, 138, 142
Sumo Indians, 40
Supreme Court, 93, 135

Talavera, Norman, 83, 111
TASS, 43
Tijerino Medrano, José Antonio, 70-71
Torres, Bernardo, 140
Torres, Lissete, 142-144
Trejos y Trejos, Félix, 70
Treminio, Guillermo, 19
Tribunals, 22
turbas divinas, 39, 57, 126, 141-142

UNESCO, 6
Union of Nicaraguan Journalists (UPN), 138
United States, 8, 129-132, 140
Urbina Lara, Jose Manuel, 22

Vega Zúñiga, Silvio, 69, 72-75
Venezuela, 10
Victoria de Julio sugar cane mill, 112
Voz de Nicaragua, La, 19-21

Walker, William, 6
Washington Post, 133
Wheelock, Jaime, 51, 138, 142
Wilson, Hector, 140
World Interparliamentary Union, 137

Zelaya Centeno, Fausto, 69
Zona Franca prison, 78

Freedom House Books

Yearbooks

Freedom in the World: Political Rights and Civil Liberties,
Raymond D. Gastil; annuals for 1978, 1979, 1980, 1981, 1982,
1983-84, 1984-85, 1985-86, 1986-87, 1987-88.

Studies in Freedom

1. *Strategies for the 1980s: Lessons of Cuba, Vietnam, and Afghanistan,*
Philip van Slyck; 1981.
2. *Escape to Freedom: The Story of the International Rescue Committee,*
Aaron Levenstein; 1983.
3. *Forty Years: A Third World Soldier at the UN,*
Carlos P. Romulo (with Beth Day Romulo); 1986. *(Romulo: A Third World Soldier at the UN,* paperback edition, 1987.)
4. *Today's American: How Free?*
James Finn & Leonard R. Sussman, (Eds.); 1986.
5. *Will of the People: Original Democracies in Non-Western Societies,*
Raul S. Manglapus; 1987.

Perspectives on Freedom

General Editor: **James Finn**

1. *El Salvador: Peaceful Revolution or Armed Struggle?,*
R. Bruce McColm; 1982.
2. *Three Years at the East-West Divide,*
Max M. Kampelman; (Introductions by Ronald Reagan and Jimmy Carter; edited by Leonard R. Sussman); 1983.
3. *The Democratic Mask: The Consolidation of the Sandinista Revolution,*
Douglas W. Payne; 1985.
4. *The Heresy of Words in Cuba: Freedom of Expression & Information,*
Carlos Ripoll; 1985.
5. *Human Rights & the New Realism: Strategic Thinking in a New Age,*
Michael Novak; 1986.
6. *To License A Journalist?,*
Inter-American Court of Human Rights; 1986.
7. *The Catholic Church in China,*
L. Ladany; 1987.
8. *Glasnost: How Open? Soviet & Eastern European Dissidents;* 1987.
9. *Yugoslavia: The Failure of "Democratic" Communism;* 1987.
10. *The Prague Spring: A Mixed Legacy*
Edited by Jiri Pehe, 1988.

Focus on Issues

1. *Big Story: How the American Press and Television Reported and Interpreted the Crisis of Tet-1968 in Vietnam and Washington,*
Peter Braestrup; Two volumes 1977;
One volume paperback abridged 1978, 1983.
2. *Soviet POWs in Afghanistan,*
Ludmilla Thorne; 1986.
3. *Afghanistan: The Great Game Revisited,*
edited by Rossane Klass; 1988.
4. *Nicaragua's Continuing Struggle: In Search of Democracy,*
Arturo J. Cruz; 1988.
5. *La Prensa: The Republic of Paper,*
Jaime Chamorro Cardenal; 1988.